Gerwyn Wise is a criminal defence barrister at Garden Court Chambers. He specialises in cases of organised crime, serious violence, sexual offences, fraud and confiscation.

Gerwyn is frequently instructed to advise and represent individuals involved in high profile cases of alleged gang activity, particularly those involving children and young adults. He has extensive experience opposing the admission of alleged gang affiliation evidence, particularly in the form of rap and drill lyrics.

Gerwyn has lectured internationally on the law relating to gang affiliation evidence, modern slavery and child trafficking. He has worked closely with organisations such as the Criminal Bar Association, Bar Council and The Law Society on drafting reforms aimed at ensuring that children and young adults are able to effectively participate in criminal trials.

Gerwyn is also the author of '*A Practical Guide to County Lines, Human Trafficking and Exploitation*'.

A Practical Guide to the Law in Relation to Gang Evidence and Drill Lyrics in Criminal Proceedings

A Practical Guide to the Law in Relation to Gang Evidence and Drill Lyrics in Criminal Proceedings

Gerwyn Wise

Barrister, Garden Court Chambers

Law Brief Publishing

Published 2025 by Law Brief Publishing, an imprint of Law Brief Publishing Ltd
30 The Parks
Minehead
Somerset
TA24 8BT

www.lawbriefpublishing.com

Paperback: 978-1-918241-07-5

FOREWORD

I have had the pleasure of knowing and working with Gerwyn for many years. I rely on his thorough preparation and insightful guidance in cases involving both children and vulnerable adults, especially those who have been exploited.

His expertise is matched by his compassion for those he represents which makes him my first choice of counsel when considering how to challenge the admissibility of gang association and musical content—particularly drill lyrics—in criminal proceedings.

Such applications often expose the pervasive systemic racism inherent in condemning individuals based on their association with drill music – a genre deeply rooted in Black cultural heritage. Music, across all forms, serves as a vital means of expression and therapy. However, artists in drill and rap face unique challenges, as their lived experiences are frequently misinterpreted or sensationalised. Recognising the therapeutic and emotional significance of their music is crucial, particularly in the context of men's mental health. Imposing restrictions on how men express emotions through music risks exacerbating these struggles, rather than addressing their root causes.

This book is an important and practical guide for legal professionals on the relevance and admissibility of gang associations and musical content. It offers clear, compelling guidance not only on the complex legal principles surrounding bad character, hearsay and expert evidence, but also on the broader societal attitudes towards Black cultural expression. By examining the methods used by police and prosecutors to link alleged gang involvement with drill music, this text tackles one of the most controversial and misunderstood areas of modern criminal law.

Thoroughly researched and thoughtfully written, this book is an essential resource for practitioners representing children and young adults in the criminal justice system. It challenges the unfounded notion that music itself drives criminal behaviour and instead draws attention to the deeper social and structural causes of crime that remain unaddressed.

By advocating for reform in how drill music is treated within the criminal justice system, this book paves the way for a fairer, more informed approach – one that recognises music as an outlet for emotion and resilience rather than a tool for condemnation.

Casey Lee Jenkins
Legal Executive Advocate at MK Law Solicitors
President of the London Criminal Courts Solicitors' Association

PREFACE

> *"...My Lords, does the Minister agree that my liking for 'The Godfather' movies make me no more or less likely to be a member of the mafia? If I am right about that, why are young black British men being prosecuted for serious violent offences in reliance on evidence of their liking for rap and drill music?"*
>
> – Baroness Chakrabarti, House of Lords debate on 25 April 2024

In recent years those of us involved in the criminal justice system have seen an upward trend in prosecution applications to adduce evidence of alleged gang affiliation. These applications are frequently based upon a defendant's interest and involvement in social media and rap music, particularly the drill genre. Indeed a significant proportion of high-profile prosecutions, almost always accusing boys and young men of serious violent offending, rely heavily on this form of evidence.

The aim of this book is to provide a practical guide to legal professionals on the relevance and admissibility of gang association and musical content, in particular drill lyrics, in criminal proceedings. This area of practice raises not only complex legal discussions about the admissibility of bad character, hearsay and expert evidence but also important societal attitudes towards black cultural heritage. Furthermore, the book will explore the various methods deployed by both the police and prosecution to restrict alleged involvement with gang activities and drill music. The growing debate in this controversial area of law is not only interesting but also necessary knowledge for any practitioner regularly instructed to represent children and young adults in criminal proceedings.

Chapter One provides an overview of how gang evidence and drill lyrics are used by both the police and prosecution.

Chapter Two sets out the recognised definitions of the term 'gang', the characteristics that practitioners should look out for in gang cases and the difficulties with identifying gang members.

Chapter Three explains the background and origin of drill music in the UK and the ways in which it is interpreted by the police and prosecution.

Chapter Four provides an overview of the bad character provisions that determine the admissibility of gang evidence. The chapter also sets out the test of admissibility established in the leading case of *Lewis* [2014] EWCA Crim 48.

Chapter Five addresses the question of relevance in accordance with the first part of the test in *Lewis* [2014] EWCA Crim 48. The chapter identifies the types of issues that are routinely considered relevant by the Court e.g. motive and the expansive approach adopted to the question in the caselaw.

Chapter Six considers the question of proving the existence and nature of a gang in accordance with the second part of the test in *Lewis* [2014] EWCA Crim 48. The chapter focuses on the caselaw relating to police officers as gang experts, the applicable rules and procedures and the steps that ought to be taken when challenging the admissibility of that evidence.

Chapter Seven considers the question of demonstrating the defendant's association or membership with the relevant gang in accordance with the third part of the test in *Lewis* [2014] EWCA Crim 48. The chapter discusses the initial restrictive approach taken by the Court of Appeal in *Alimi* [2014] EWCA Crim 2412 to the question of gang membership, but goes on to detail the subsequent caselaw that approached the issue in a more expansive manner.

Chapter Eight addresses the question of fairness and exclusion of gang evidence in accordance with the fourth and final part of the test in *Lewis* [2014] EWCA Crim 48. The chapter considers the approach taken by the Court to the balancing exercise between the probative value of the evidence against the prejudicial effect of admitting it against the defendant. The chapter also discusses the approach to be taken to legal directions if the gang evidence is held to be admissible.

Chapter Nine provides an overview of the recent adoption by both the police and the prosecution of civil injunctions and orders to regulate the behaviour of those allegedly involved in gangs. The chapter discusses the use of gang injunctions and criminal behaviour orders to restrict the involvement of individuals in drill music.

Chapter Ten details the relevant law in relation to applications for gang injunctions. The chapter focuses particularly on the statutory two stage test, the burden and standard of proof, the type of evidence adduced in support of the applications and the relevance of the European Convention on Human Rights.

Chapter Eleven details the relevant law in relation to applications for criminal behaviour orders. The chapter focuses on the statutory framework, the two specific conditions required to impose the order, the types or prohibitions and requirements included within the orders and how practitioners ought to respond to applications.

Chapter Twelve suggests potential reforms to the treatment of gang evidence and drill music in criminal proceedings, particularly focusing on evidential thresholds, standards for experts and jury directions.

The law within this book is up to date to the time of drafting on 1 October 2025.

Gerwyn Wise
October 2025

CONTENTS

PART ONE

OVERVIEW AND DEFINITIONS

CHAPTER ONE

INTRODUCTION TO GANG EVIDENCE AND DRILL LYRICS

Evidence of alleged gang association and membership, frequently presented in the form of drill lyrics and videos, has formed the basis for an increasing number of criminal prosecutions in recent years.

Lyrics and music videos, often posted by young teenage boys on social media platforms such as YouTube, Instagram and Snapchat, are frequently relied upon by the prosecution to demonstrate gang affiliation, criminal intent and even confessions to criminal behaviour. The case is often put that the young defendant has used social media and drill music to promote gang culture and to glamourise the gang lifestyle. For example, this is often said to be demonstrated in videos or lyrics that comment on specific incidents of gang violence, possession of and use of weapons and the making of threats towards police officers or rival gang members.

The admission in criminal cases of gang evidence, in particular rap and drill music, has proved controversial. Legal practitioners working in this area will know that evidence of gang affiliation is almost always relied upon by the prosecution in cases involving serious violence, weapons and drugs, particularly where the case is based on so called 'joint enterprise' i.e. secondary liability. Most defendants in these cases are young men, frequently in their teens, and significantly they are almost exclusively of black ethnicity. Consequently, alleged gang association evidence is disproportionately used in trials involving young black men and boys. For those of us working in this area of law, the criticism is often heard that the overreliance on such evidence, in particular drill music, has resulted in an attack on black culture and unfair stereotyping of young black men and boys as gang members.

It is certainly the case that evidence of alleged gang association, presented in the form of social media comments, music videos and drill lyrics, is frequently extracted and interpreted by individuals from backgrounds very different to those charged with offences e.g. police officers. While this form of evidence may be probative in some cases, the nature and content of drill music can be shocking to juries and it is often argued that its admission would be highly prejudicial, not only for the defendant that it may relate to but also for co-defendants in the trial. As discussed in this book, although there has been a numerical increase of appeals heard on the point in recent years, there has been limited successful challenge in the Court of Appeal to the prosecution's use of gang evidence and drill lyrics in criminal proceedings. Furthermore, both the police and the prosecution regularly seek, and are almost always granted, civil injunctions and post-conviction orders by the Court to control the involvement of certain artists in the drill music scene.

For practitioners instructed in these cases, there are a series of questions that often must be grappled with and which this book will seek to address:

- How does the Court assess the probative value of gang evidence, particularly cultural and musical material?
- When is such evidence found by the Court to be inadmissible?
- What are the proper limits of expert commentary on gang evidence and drill music?
- How should practitioners draft applications to exclude gang evidence?

- Are the principles of necessity and proportionality relevant when opposing police and prosecution applications for civil injunctions and post-conviction orders?

Legal practitioners working in this area need a complete understanding of the relevant legislation, case law and, perhaps more significantly, strategic tools that are essential when identifying and challenging the evidential use of such material in criminal proceedings.

CHAPTER TWO

DEFINITION OF A 'GANG'

For practitioners instructed in criminal cases involving gang related investigations, much will depend on the approach taken by the parties and the Court to the interpretation of key terms, particularly the 'gang'.

Academic and legal definitions

The Eurogang Project, a network of international youth group / gang experts and researchers, defined the street gang as "*any durable, street-oriented youth group whose identity includes involvement in legal activity.*" This is widely regarded as the leading definition and is used by gang experts and researchers around the word, including in the UK.

In a 2009 report, the definition was largely adopted by a working group of UK experts at The Centre for Social Justice, who proposed the following general definition:

> "*A relatively durable, predominantly street-based group of young people who (1) see themselves (and are seen by others) as a discernible group, (2) engage in a range of criminal activity and violence, (3) identify with or lay claim over territory (4) have some form of identifying structural feature, and (5) are in conflict with other, similar gangs.*"

> The Centre for Social Justice, '*Dying to Belong*', February 2009

Unfortunately there is no universal legal definition of the term 'gang' within the criminal justice system of England and Wales. This is despite often substantial use of the term by the police, prosecution and judiciary in criminal cases.

It is worth noting that the term 'gang-related' does appear in primary legislation. Under s.34(5) of the Policing and Crime Act 2009 ('PCA 2009'), behaviour is considered 'gang-related' if it occurred in the course of, or was otherwise related to, the activities of a group that:

(a) Consisted of at least three people, and

(b) Had one or more characteristics that enabled its members to be identified by others as a group.

The type of activities that the legislation envisaged were "*engaging in or encouraging or assisting gang-related violence or gang related drug-dealing activity*" (s.34(3) PCA 2009). While the PCA 2009 provides some assistance, it is a definition drafted exclusively for the purpose of determining civil applications for gang injunctions. It amounts to a very broad definition and was undoubtedly drafted having regard for the lower evidential thresholds applicable within the civil law framework of injunctions. Unsurprisingly it has not been adopted as the standard in criminal proceedings. For a full discussion of the law and procedure in relation to gang injunctions see Chapter 10.

Characteristics of a 'gang'

The police and prosecution frequently point to certain characteristics when seeking to prove both the existence of a gang and an individual's association or membership of that gang.

The starting point will normally be evidence of self-identification and association by a group of individuals with a particular territory or apparent gang name. The alleged gang will often, but not always, have incorporated a post code area or housing estate into their identification e.g. Woolwich Boys, London Fields, E5 etc. Identification of the gang may be demonstrated by members wearing particular colours, making specific hand signs or gestures, and the drawing of graffiti tags. Furthermore, practitioners working in this area will often be presented with videos and images from social media platforms in which the police and prosecution claim the material shows an association between the individual and a particular gang.

The prosecution frequently relies upon evidence of previous criminal behaviour, whether it resulted in conviction or not, to assist with establishing both the existence of the gang and the individual's membership of the gang. The root cause of much gang activity is unquestionably drug supply. Evidence of an individual's previous involvement in drug supply, particularly if linked with other alleged gang members, inevitably forms part of prosecution submissions. Members of gangs frequently carry weapons, both for protection and to engage in retaliatory attacks on rival gangs. Therefore, previous incidents in which the individual has been found in possession of weapons, ranging from small knives to machetes, will often be set out in prosecution applications. For a period a few years ago the carrying of acid and other corrosive substances also frequently formed part of prosecution submissions on gang membership. However, such submissions have largely fallen away in recent years following a significant drop off in incidents of so called 'acid attacks', largely credited to the imposition of lengthy prison sentences in high profile cases for individuals convicted of such attacks.

When considering evidence in support of the existence of a gang and potential membership, the Court is often presented with evidence of county lines drug operations being overseen by senior gang members. These enterprises are highly profitable, 24/7 businesses that rely upon the exploitation of others. The individuals targeted for recruitment into these operations are almost always either children or vulnerable adults. This is because they are most susceptible to the exploitation techniques used by the organisers of the drugs line. Legal practitioners working in this area will have had experience advising children recruited because of their special educational needs, mental health issues, disabilities, absent / busy parents or guardians, homelessness or previous convictions; essentially children that the recruiters believe can be easily extracted from pre-existing support networks. The recruitment is often based on a glamourisation of the gang lifestyle, with current members presented in videos and photographs on social media in possession of large amounts of cash, designer clothes and jewellery. The prosecution frequently relies upon this material, not only against those appearing in the videos and photographs, but also against those who have been sent this material as part of the recruitment exercise, to establish either association with or membership of a particular gang.

Difficulties with identifying a 'gang'

Legal practitioners instructed in these cases ought to be alert to the dangers of unconscious bias when considering whether there is sufficient evidence of both the existence of the gang and an individual's membership of it. Gang affiliation and membership is frequently fluid and inconsistent. Large friendship groups of teenagers may include individuals involved in their own, personal criminal activity which is unrelated to others in the wider group. The use of a postcode by a group of individuals to identify themselves may be entirely innocent and designed to show an affinity or association with a particular area, much like supporting the local football team.

When speaking with boys and young men accused of gang membership the position is often complicated. Many individuals state that the names of the so called gangs have been given to them by those same police officers. They often say that the gang names and street tags relied upon extensively by the police and prosecution are not even used by the individuals identified in these applications. Therefore, legal practitioners should start by questioning how much of the labelled gang activity is due to the misapplication of naming and/or grouping together of boys and young men who happen to congregate in a particular public space. The question must always be whether there is credible evidence to support an assertion that a particular group is a 'gang' and that the identified individual is an established associate or member of it.

It is important to approach these questions of gang association and membership forensically and with care. The labelling of an individual or group of individuals, particularly young black men and boys, as 'gang members' inevitably leads to negative stereotyping. Experience teaches those of us working in this area that the indiscriminate use of the 'gang' label has the potential to have a profound impact on such young people; too often the evidence relied upon by the police and prosecution risks equating social and cultural associations with evidence of criminal activity. We see this in the approach taken to drill lyrics and videos. In addition to the risk of racial stereotyping, we have seen the impact of an overly broad approach taken to the definition of the 'gang' in so called 'joint enterprise' prosecutions, as the net of criminal liability is frequently extended far beyond that which can be established by other evidence.

For a demonstration of the dangers involved in a broad brush approach to the issue of gang membership, look no further than the Metropolitan Police gang matrix. It was introduced following the aftermath of the riots in London in 2011, an event that politicians largely blamed, without foundation, on gang activity. The aim of the gang matrix was to reduce gang-related violence by keeping a record of relevant London gang members. It was essentially a risk assessment tool principally used by the Metropolitan Police to rank London's suspected gang members according to their propensity for violence. The individuals, or 'gang nominals' as they were described, were marked in a traffic light scoring system; red for those most likely to commit violent crimes. To encourage a multi-agency approach to tackling gangs, the data was shared with other organisations including local authorities, youth offending teams, probation service, health agencies, housing associations and educational establishments.

For those of us working in this area, the gang matrix proved not only ineffective but it clearly discriminated against young black men and boys. Unsurprisingly, given the lack of an agreed legal definition for a 'gang', the criteria for being listed on the gang matrix was vague and was applied inconsistently throughout the different boroughs of London. Those deciding on listing relied upon not only previous criminal history, but also social media content, friendship groups, associations and unverifiable intelligence from police officers, third party agencies and members of the local community. Many of the indicators used to identify gang members simply reflected elements of typical youth culture, such as an interest in drill music, and had nothing to do with an involvement in criminal activities. By conflating culture with criminal behaviour, the criteria resulted in a heavily racialised approach; young black men and boys were disproportionately listed on the gang matrix, resulting in the inevitable disenfranchisement and isolation of some of the most vulnerable young people in society. Furthermore, the sharing of the gang matrix data with other government agencies meant that the stigmatising effect of being identified as a 'gang nominal' followed those listed in their interactions with other service providers in health, housing, education and employment. Having been criticised as not only ineffective but counterproductive, the Metropolitan Police gang matrix was discontinued on 13 February 2024.

The flaws at the heart of the Metropolitan Police's gang matrix provide a stark warning to legal practitioners working in this area; a cautious approach must be deployed when approaching the question of gangs and gang membership. In an encouraging development, the Court of Appeal recently warned against the generalised use of and reference to groups of individuals as a gang. In *Oni and others* [2025] EWCA Crim 12, Lord Justice Dingemans stated at paragraph 14:

> *"it is obviously important in any case to ensure that separate individuals are not unfairly treated as one entity, and that groups of friends or individuals sharing an interest in music are not unfairly labelled as gangs."*

Moving forward, legal practitioners instructed to represent individuals accused of gang membership ought to have this comment at the forefront of any submissions made in response to overly broad police and prosecution applications.

CHAPTER THREE

DRILL MUSIC IN THE UK

Drill is a music genre marked by aggressive lyrics and frequent references to violence, drugs, weapons and street life.

It originated in Chicago but made its way to the UK in the early 2010s. The UK version developed a distinctive form, growing and developing a particular style principally within groups of young black people living in London. In recent years, drill has entered the mainstream and has become a regular feature of the entertainment and music industry in the UK.

Drill artists adopt stage names, sometimes unfairly described as a street or gang name by the police. They wear particular fashions e.g. balaclavas, tracksuits, puffer jackets. In videos accompanying drill songs, groups of young men with housing estate backdrops use their hands to mimic weapons, letters and symbols sometimes associated with local gangs; it is not unusual for those appearing in these videos to produce weapons such as knives and machetes.

An exaggerated, hypermasculine persona forms part of the genre's performance style. This is reflected in the lyrics that typically seek to highlight the lived realities of young people living in deprived areas, which sometimes refer to real life events. However, lyrics are more often fictional or metaphorical, relying upon exaggerated themes to enhance the material. Legal practitioners working in this area will know that drill lyrics are intentionally shocking, provocative and frequently rely upon hyperbole. It is a feature of the genre that the artist projects an authentic persona of an individual ready and willing to engage in violence. In some cases the artist raps about a real criminal act they may have committed. However, while the appearance of authenticity is key, many of those involved in the production of drill lyrics and videos have no connection at all with criminal activities.

Nevertheless, the police and prosecution have sought in recent years to rely upon such material, obtained from social media platforms such as Instagram, Snapchat, YouTube and TikTok, to evidence an association with both gang and criminal activities. The content of the lyrics and associated videos is often used to try and demonstrate a propensity for violence, pre-existing hostility towards rival gangs, motive for a particular offence and even post-offence confessions. But the material obtained by the police is often decontextualised, selectively disclosed and inevitably misunderstood. The so-called experts tasked with interpreting and decoding lyrics for judges and juries are almost always police officers; the expertise is often based upon their own viewing of a significant number of videos on YouTube which it is claimed gives them a special knowledge of the material. But police officer 'experts' frequently adopt an overly literal reading of the lyrics, creating the risk of evidential overreach rooted in both cultural and generational misunderstanding.

Indeed as Lord Justice Legatt warned at paragraph 15 of the Court of Appeal ruling in *Soloman* [2019] EWCA Crim 1356, when attaching little weight or significance to drill lyrics found on the appellant's mobile telephone, "*...lyrics of a song do not necessarily or perhaps commonly bear a connection with actual real life events.*" This ought to be the starting point for any legal practitioner when faced with police and prosecution applications relying upon drill lyrics and videos.

PART 2

ADMISSIBILITY OF GANG EVIDENCE IN CRIMINAL CASES

CHAPTER FOUR

OVERVIEW OF THE LEGISLATIVE FRAMEWORK AND LEWIS [2014] EWCA CRIM 48

In England and Wales, the use of gang evidence has developed under the broad framework of the bad character provisions introduced under the Criminal Justice Act 2003 ('CJA 2003'). Legal practitioners are routinely presented with gang evidence in a range of cases, in particular the prosecution of young black men and boys accused of serious violence, drug dealing and public disorder.

The source of gang evidence varies from case to case but typically includes incidents of previous gang related activities, police gang intelligence reports, photographs and videos showing an association with gang related symbols or colours and, particularly in recent years, drill lyrics and videos. The material is typically reduced into a witness statement produced by a police officer described by the prosecution as a gang expert. Prosecutors frequently seek to rely upon this gang evidence to prove a motive for the alleged crime, to establish an association between defendants, to link a defendant to a particular location, group or event and, significantly, to support a theory of joint enterprise gang offending.

The material rarely provides direct proof of an element of the alleged offence; more often it is described as providing a level of background detail to assist the jury, which legal practitioners working in this area need to be ready to carefully scrutinise and challenge.

Legislative Framework

Almost all gang material is advanced by the prosecution as bad character evidence, specifically that it is "*evidence of, or a disposition towards, misconduct*" (s.98 CJA 2003). The only exception is where the gang material either 'has to do with' the facts of the offence or is given 'in connection with' the investigation or prosecution of the offence.

Under s.112(1) CJA 2003, the term 'misconduct' is defined as the "*commission of an offence or other reprehensible conduct*". Given alleged gang evidence is often presented by the prosecution as 'reprehensible' behaviour requiring satisfaction of one of the legislative gateways, the characterisation of the material as bad character is rarely challenged by defence practitioners. But should that be the default position in relation to rap and drill music?

The term 'reprehensible' was considered by the Court of Appeal in *Renda* [2005] EWCA Crim 2826. In that case one of several appellants argued that the judge at first instance had been mistaken when allowing the prosecution to adduce, as bad character, evidence that he had previously been found unfit to plead to an assault matter and had received an absolute discharge after a finding of fact was made against him. At paragraph 24 of the judgment, Sir Igor Judge, the then President of the Queen's Bench Division, accepted that an absolute discharge following a finding that a defendant was unfit to plead would not amount to either a criminal conviction or reprehensible conduct. He stated, "*as a matter of ordinary language, the word 'reprehensible' carries with it some element of culpability or blameworthiness.*"

The question then becomes 'what is reprehensible about drill lyrics or videos?' It is rare for either the prosecution or the judge to specify what aspect of the music is said to be reprehensible when addressing these applications. It cannot sensibly be argued that the act of writing or performing drill music amounts to reprehensible behaviour. Therefore, the reprehensible behaviour must be said to be the individual's interest in, production of or performance of music that addresses topics of violence, weapons, drugs and gang activity. If that is the case, the question should be asked 'what about individuals who are interested in or produce or perform in violent films, television shows or plays?' What is it that sets rap and drill music apart from those other cultural activities? Is it that rap and drill music is a form of cultural expression primarily performed by young black men and boys who fit a stereotypical image of the criminal gang member?

Legal practitioners instructed in these cases need to be prepared to challenge such stereotypes and assumptions. However, the point isn't often argued simply because it is believed that the defence is afforded extra protection by accepting the 'bad character' description as admissibility depends not only relevance but also satisfaction of one of the seven gateways under s.101(a) CJA 2003. However, as set out in subsequent chapters, the gateways very rarely provide much of an obstacle to the admission of such evidence i.e. rap and drill music assessed as relevant almost always satisfies one of the statutory gateways.

If, as is normally the position, the gang material is held to fall under the bad character provisions, admissibility is typically covered under two of the statutory gateways:

- Gateway C – it is important explanatory evidence (s.101(1)(c) CJA 2003)

- Gateway D – it is relevant to an important matter in issue between the defendant and the prosecution (s.101(1)(d) CJA 2003)

It is worth noting that the prosecution occasionally advances these applications on the basis that the relevant gang evidence 'has to do with' the facts of the offence and is therefore admissible under s.98 CJA 2003. This issue was addressed in detail by the Court of Appeal in *Sule* [2012] EWCA Crim 1130.

In Sule the prosecution had sought to admit evidence of 'tit-for-tat' gang violence in the three months preceding the incident leading to the murder. The material was said to be relevant to motive and the judge ruled it admissible on the basis that it was 'to do' with the alleged facts of the offence. Counsel on behalf of the appellant argued in the Court of Appeal that the material should not have been admitted as there was an insufficient nexus of time between the previous incidents and the alleged offence. The appellant relied upon the comments of the Court of Appeal in the earlier case of *Tirnaveanu* [2007] EWCA Crim 1239, in which Lord Justice Thomas at paragraph 23 stated that the s.98 exclusion "*must be related to evidence where there is some nexus in time between the offence with which the defendant is charged and the evidence of misconduct which the prosecution seeks to adduce*". The Court of Appeal in *Sule* dismissed the appeal stating that s.98 did not include any "*express or obviously implicit temporal qualification*" (paragraph 11), but even if it did the prosecution would have satisfied such a hurdle in that case. The decision in *Tirnaveanu* was distinguished on the basis that the evidence sought to be relied upon did not concern motive.

The decision in *Sule* opened the door for gang evidence linked to motive to be admitted even though it related to matters that occurred a considerable time, months even years, before the alleged offence. Furthermore, the broad approach taken to the scope of s.98 CJA 2003 conferred an extensive discretion on trial judges when deciding upon the admissibility of gang evidence; it may be found to be admissible under the s.98 exclusion or through the bad character gateways. Indeed, the Court of Appeal in *Sule* acknowledged this point and referred with approval to the comments of Professor J R Spencer QC which were considered at paragraph 24 in *Tirnaveanu*:

> "*We respectfully agree with Professor J R Spencer QC Evidence of Bad Character, para 2.23, where he suggests that there is a potential overlap between evidence that has to do with the alleged facts of the offence and evidence that might be admitted through one of the gateways in section 101(1). As he observes in relation to the example he took of prior*

misconduct being the reason for the commission of the offence , such evidence could be admitted either as 'to do' with the offence or as important explanatory evidence under section 101(1)(c) of the CJA 2003 : 'In practice nothing of any legal significance depends on which of these two routes it is by which the evidence comes in."

That has been the approach in practice of trial judges, which has been upheld in several Court of Appeal cases (see *Heslop* [2022] EWCA Crim 897 and *Stewart* [2016] EWCA Crim 447). Legal practitioners working in this area will have had experience of the Court 'hedging its bets' when making decisions on the admissibility of gang evidence. Frequently trial judges accept that the evidence may be admissible under s.98 CJA 2003 but nevertheless move on and conclude that one or more of the statutory gateways has equally been satisfied by the prosecution.

If the Court concludes that the applicant has satisfied one of the gateways, there remains a residual power to exclude the material on grounds of fairness either under s.101(3) CJA 2003 or s.78 of the Police and Criminal Evidence Act 1984 ('PACE 1984').

The test for admissibility in *Lewis*

As discussed in previous chapters, the use of gang evidence in criminal trials has proved controversial and has attracted significant criticism. While such evidence can sometimes provide useful and important context, in almost every case there is a significant risk of prejudice to the defendant. Indeed the Court of Appeal recognised the inevitable prejudicial effect of gang evidence *Awoyemi* [2016] EWCA Crim 668, where Lady Justice Hallett warned at paragraph 26 of the judgment that "*evidence of gang affiliation is by its very nature highly prejudicial and great care should be taken before a trial judge allows it into evidence.*"

Nevertheless, such material frequently forms the basis of prosecution bad character applications. In the leading case of *Lewis* [2014] EWCA Crim 48, the Court of Appeal provided guidance about the circumstances in which gang material may be put before the jury. In that case the various appellants appealed against convictions for several offences arising out of an incident of public disorder in Birmingham. The prosecution's case had been that the appellants were part of a masked group who had broken into a public house, set it on fire and had shot at police officers when they attended the scene. The issues for the jury included identification of those present, whether there had been an innocent explanation for their presence and links to firearms. To establish gang association, pro-firearm views and anti-police tendencies, the prosecution successfully applied to adduce bad character evidence that included videos of the appellants engaging in gang related activities.

In relation to the convictions that followed the trial, the main ground of appeal common to all appellants was that the judge had erred in admitting the bad character evidence. Sir Brian Leveson, the then President of the Queen's Bench Division, confirmed that any decision about the admissibility of alleged gang evidence sought under s.101(1)(d) CJA 2003 would need to address the following four questions (paragraph 82):

> (1) *Is the evidence relevant to an important matter in issue between a defendant and the prosecution?*
>
> (2) *Is there proper evidence of the existence and nature of the gang or gangs?*
>
> (3) *Does the evidence, if accepted, go to show the defendant was a member of or associated with a gang or gangs which exhibited violence or hostility to the police or with links with firearms?*
>
> (4) *If the evidence is admitted, will it have such an adverse effect on the fairness of the proceedings that it ought to be excluded?*

The *Lewis* test created a four-point structure for the admissibility of gang evidence. It is worth noting that the Court of Appeal in *Awoyemi* [2016] EWCA Crim 668 clarified that Sir Brian Leveson in *Lewis* was not laying down four questions that must be asked in every case but instead "*took the principles from the statute and applied them to the facts of the case*" (paragraph 35). Nevertheless, the four questions have been adopted as a useful guide to practitioners when considering the admissibility of gang evidence.

The subsequent chapters consider each question in turn. However, legal practitioners working in this area will know that both trial judges and the Court of Appeal have been very slow to conclude that evidence of gang material in some form should not go before the jury.

CHAPTER FIVE

LEWIS QUESTION 1: IS THE EVIDENCE RELEVANT?

In the Privy Council case of *Myers* [2015] UKPC 40, which concerned the admissibility of gang evidence in the Bermuda jurisdiction, Lord Hughes summarised the fundamental principles of admissibility and relevance in the following way (paragraph 37):

> *"The starting point is that evidence is not admissible unless it is relevant. It is relevant if, but only if, it contributes something to the resolution of one or more of the issues in the case. It may do so either directly or indirectly."*

As outlined in the previous chapter, the Court of Appeal in *Lewis* [2014] EWCA Crim 48 confirmed that the first question for legal practitioners tasked with considering the admissibility of gang evidence and drill lyrics is whether the material is relevant to a live issue in the case. There was no question in *Lewis* that evidence demonstrating membership or association with a gang was of potential relevance. This followed a series of earlier cases in which evidence of gang association, even when limited to circumstantial material, was admitted as relevant under the bad character provisions.

In *Elliott* [2010] EWCA Crim 2378, evidence showing that the appellant was a gang member involved in drug and gun crime was held to have been properly admitted as relevant to an important matter in issue under s.101(1)(d) CJA 2003. In that case, the police had found drugs and firearms in a cupboard directly outside the appellant's home address. He denied knowledge and possession of those items during the trial. The prosecution was given permission by the Court to present evidence of the appellant's alleged gang membership, specifically in the form of letters referring to his interest and involvement with a gang and images recovered from his mobile phone showing him making a hand gesture forming the gang's distinctive sign. In dismissing the appeal, the Court of Appeal stated that "*evidence which could satisfy them that the applicant was a member of a gang which was involved in drug crime and in the carrying or use of firearms was plainly capable of assisting the jury to reach its decision*" given the issue was knowledge of the drugs and guns.

Relevant Issues

A careful review of the Court of Appeal authorities shows that gang evidence, in particular drill lyrics and videos, are routinely found to be relevant to several different trial issues.

Motive

The first and most frequently identified issue tends to be motive, in particular gang retaliation.

That was the issue identified in the Privy Council case of *Myers.* Each of the three cases heard in *Myers* concerned a deliberate shooting by someone who had sought out the victim. Two of the victims were shot dead; the third was hit but survived. The issue in each case was the identity of the shooters. In two of the trials the prosecution adduced evidence that the shooting was part of a long-standing feud between two rival gangs and was triggered by an incident shortly beforehand. In the third trial the gang evidence was admitted in consequence of cross-examination of the surviving victim, not to prove the existence of a feud between identifiable gangs but to prove loyalty in the gang between the appellant and an associate who had been insulted. Thus in each of the cases the gang evidence was admitted principally to demonstrate that each appellant had a motive to kill the respective victim.

The appeal was refused. In the judgment Lord Hughes started from the position that evidence of motive will always be relevant even though it will not be necessary for the prosecution to prove it (paragraph 43). He stated:

> "*…where there is evidence that the defendant had a motive to kill the victim, that goes to support the case that it was him, rather than someone else, and/or that he did it with murderous intent, rather than accidentally or without intent to do at least grievous bodily harm. It may equally be relevant to rebut asserted self-defence or provocation. Admissible evidence of motive may sometimes necessarily involve showing bad behaviour by the defendant on occasions other than that charged.*"

In *Myers*, each of the three appellants had advanced a defence that they were not responsible for the shootings and that there was no explanation for why they would have been involved. The evidence of gang association was admitted to rebut those defences and to support their identifications as the gunmen. In relation to the first two appellants, Lord Hughes described the evidence of gang association as "*an important strand in the rope of evidence that there had occurred a trigger event which would have created a grievance in the gang of which the defendant was a member*" (paragraph 49). In relation to the third appellant, although there was no evidence of a triggering event or gang warfare, evidence of previous hostility between an associate of the appellant and the victim provided support for a motive. It is worth noting that the Court of Appeal has more recently confirmed that there is no requirement for there to have been a "*trigger event*" in such cases (see paragraph 44 of *Heslop* [2022] EWCA Crim 897).

In the case of *Sode* [2017] EWCA Crim 705 the Court of Appeal upheld a rather broad assessment of relevance in the context of motive. The three appellants appealed against their convictions at the Central Criminal Court for joint enterprise murder and possession of a firearm with intent to cause fear of violence. The prosecution case was that all three were members of the Anti-Shower and Monson Road gang, that they had taken part in a fatal shooting of a member of the rival Shower Gang and the killing had been a revenge attack for an incident that had previously occurred. The three appellants argued that the trial judge had erred in admitting evidence of previous 'tit-for-tat' violence between the two gangs, which included one of the appellants appearing in a YouTube video filmed two years before the shooting in which the then 14 year old appellant made a gesture and remarks supportive of the Anti-Shower Gang.

The appeals were refused. In the judgment at paragraph 48, Lady Justice Hallett stated that the Court was in no doubt that the gang affiliation evidence was relevant because the shooting "*bore all the hallmarks*" of a gang-related revenge attack. She went on to address the relevance of the gang evidence, including the YouTube video. At paragraph 53 Lady Justice Hallett stated that it went to motive and that the "*video provided a clear and direct link between Green and the Anti-Shower Gang, rivals of the Shower Gang, of which the deceased was a member.*" This conclusion was reached despite counsel for the appellant having made the point that the video amounted to little more than the then 14 year old appellant 'freestyling' over 2 years before the incident. The Court of Appeal found that the two year gap did not "*reduce its impact or diminish its relevance.*"

Intent

As outlined by Lord Hughes in *Myers*, gang evidence is not only relevant to the issue of motive. It is frequently admitted to assist juries in their assessment of the defendant's statement of mind, specifically his intention.

In *O* [2010] EWCA Crim 2985 the appellant was convicted of possessing a firearm and ammunition with intent to endanger life. The police had stopped a minicab and found the appellant in the front passenger seat with a loaded firearm in the footwell. The prosecution sought to rely on evidence that the appellant was a member of a violent gang in south

London. The evidence included a YouTube video recorded 6 months before his arrest showing the appellant rapping with others and using the words '*mack*', '*nine*' and '*got the ting cocked*', which the prosecution stated were references to guns. The appellant accepted that he was rapping in the video, that any references to guns and violence were metaphorical and that it was part of 10 further videos that had been created by him in a commercial studio to gain the attention of a record producer.

The trial judge allowed the prosecution to present the evidence before the jury. Although they acknowledged that the trial judge had not fully explained his reasoning, the Court of Appeal stated that the gang evidence was clearly admitted under s.101(1)(d) CJA 2003 as "*it would have made it more likely that the appellant was guilty of the offence of possessing the weapon with the intent alleged*" if accepted by the jury (paragraph 17). The Court of Appeal had no concerns about either the 6 month gap between recording and arrest or the lack of any mention in the lyrics to specific threats or persons (paragraph 25). The reasoning in *O* is thought by legal practitioners to represent a broad interpretation of the relevance test.

Presence and association

The prosecution frequently applies to admit evidence of gang membership when seeking to establish both presence and association of defendants with the crime and others involved. That was the prosecution position in *Lewis*.

In *Lewis* the prosecution had successfully argued that the appearance of several appellants in music videos found on YouTube were relevant to important matters in issue during the trial. The prosecution asserted that the videos helped to prove the appellant's presence around the pub at the time of the violence, that their presence was not innocent and that they had a common purpose to commit the unlawful acts. Having identified the four important trial issues as "*common purpose, identification, innocent presence and firearms*", the Court of Appeal concluded at paragraph 87 that:

> *"...the evidence in question was of potential relevance to each of the four issues set out by the prosecution. The judge was certainly entitled to conclude it was relevant in the case of a defendant who disputed that he was there, and in the case of a defendant who said, in effect, 'I was there by chance'."*

Legal practitioners working in this area will be aware of the earlier decision in *Saleem* [2007] EWCA Crim 1923, where lyrics formed the basis for a similar decision.

In *Saleem* the appellant sought to challenge his conviction for causing grievous bodily harm with intent arising out of an alleged joint enterprise plan and attack conducted with others. He had been present at the time of the attack but claimed that he had no prior knowledge or participation of the assault i.e. innocent presence. The prosecution case was that the appellant was part of the planned attack, it was his 17th birthday and he had attended to take photographs of the attack to show others. During a search of the appellant's bedroom the police had found photographs on his computer showing victims of previous assaults along with 2000 files relating to rap lyrics and music; this included five pages of lyrics that had been downloaded but altered by the appellant to include the following paragraph:

> *"Im gon make history, 1stly dey gon call me mister an dey gon say I dissed ya, I hav 2 b carfull hu I talk 2 becos ur bird wil be da listner, 2ndly February 24th my birth day im gon make it ur worst day, 3rdly do I have 2 have u layin in emergency 2 have dem stitch ya?"*

The prosecution argued that both the photographs and the lyrics ought to be admitted to rebut his defence of innocent presence, particularly the lyrics that referred to the appellant planning to assault someone on his birthday (which was the date of the incident). In relation to the rap lyrics, the appellant's team argued that the evidence showed that they had been downloaded on 7 November 2004 and the file containing the edited version above had last been accessed 10 days before the incident on 13 February 2005 and was therefore clearly not relevant. The judge ruled that both the photographs and the lyrics were relevant to rebutting the defence case of innocent presence.

The Court of Appeal agreed with the judge and stated that the evidence was "*relevant to rebutting the case of innocent presence*" (paragraph 27) and was therefore admissible under s.101(1)(d) CJA 2003. The timing point raised by the appellant was noted but was held to be a "*factor that went to weight rather than relevance*". The Court of Appeal did acknowledge though that the significant gap in time between the creation/amending of the lyrics and the offence meant that the lyrics could not be admissible as 'to do with the facts of the offence' under s.98 CJA 2003 or as a motive because they were "*not sufficiently connected with the facts of the offence*" (paragraph 32).

The rationale of the Court of Appeal is not very easy to follow. The lyrics did not discuss the offence. The lyrics did not establish a motive. The lyrics were not close in time to the offence. The relevance, if there was any, appears to be the reference to the appellant's birthday and suggestion that he would commit violence that day, which was the date of the incident. That appears to have been the basis for the Court of Appeal's reasoning when upholding the trial judge's decision. It would seem, although it is not clear at all from the judgment, that the Court of Appeal may have reached a different conclusion if there had either been no mention of the birthday in the lyrics or if the incident had occurred on a date other than the appellant's birthday.

Expansive interpretation of relevance

The Court of Appeal has concluded in almost every reported case that gang evidence, particularly in the form of rap and drill music, was relevant for the particular purpose advanced by the prosecution. There is very little evidence of it being persuaded by submissions addressing the complexities, cultural conventions and commercial drivers of rap and drill music, specifically the danger associated with undertaking a literal interpretation of lyrics and videos. This point is best illustrated by the Court of Appeal's judgment in *Awoyemi* [2016] EWCA Crim 668.

In *Awoyemi*, the three appellants were convicted of attempted murder and possessing a firearm with intent to endanger life in relation to a shooting. The appellants lived in Dagenham and were alleged to have been members of the DAG gang. The prosecution alleged that the target of the shooting was intended to be a member of the Beckton Boys gang. The judge allowed the prosecution to adduce evidence of the appellants' alleged affiliation to the DAG gang on the basis that the initial shooting and the attempt to finish the job two weeks later bore the hallmarks of gang violence. The evidence of gang affiliation included handwritten rap lyrics referring to violence, drugs, guns and the DAG gang and YouTube videos showing two of the appellants making gun gestures with their hands and rapping "*don't fuck with my family. Why? Cos I'll be eager to let slug fly*". The prosecution application had been resisted by the defence principally on the basis that there was no evidence at all of any dispute between the DAG gang and the Beckton Boys, notwithstanding the appellants having made it clear that their ties to members of the DAG gang were historical through school, youth groups and football training. Therefore, and this point was advanced in the Court of Appeal, the gang material was not relevant because there was no or insufficient evidence that the shooting and / or possession of the firearm were gang related.

The Court of Appeal disagreed. At paragraphs 32 and 33 of the judgment, Lady Justice Hallett stated:

> "*We are entirely satisfied the evidence of gang affiliation was relevant and admissible on the facts of this case. The shooting, and the return visit to finish the job, bore all the hallmarks of gang related violence. On the first occasion two cars travelled in convoy to an address considered home territory by another gang. Someone fired through a door, reckless as to who might be the other side, no doubt in an attempt*

> *both to kill and to terrify. On the second occasion, one of the same cars with three occupants equipped with balaclavas, a bandana and a loaded shotgun (the same gun available for use by members of a gang) headed towards the same scene.*
>
> *... In each case, the gang affiliation evidence provided a link between them and a gang that gloried in violence and the use of firearms, mourned murdered friends and threatened violent retribution for those who crossed them. The Crown could thereby establish a possible motive for the shooting, an association with firearms and lethal violence, and could negative innocent presence and association. The evidence was prejudicial but inevitably so and not unduly so. It went far beyond simple membership of a gang, the love of RAP music, hyperbole or appearance on a video. It indicated the extent to which the individuals concerned had signed up to gang and gun culture."*

The Court of Appeal essentially concluded that the incident was clearly gang related and therefore the gang evidence was relevant to address issues of motive, links with firearms / violence and to rebut innocent presence and association. Legal practitioners again may question why the Court of Appeal was able to confidently conclude that the incident was gang related rather than something else entirely; the use of firearms, the movement of vehicles, the targeting of premises is not obviously exclusive to gang behaviour and frequently arises in non-gang cases. As part of her broad approach to the issue of relevance, Lady Justice Hallet rejected the suggestion that gang evidence was not relevant because the prosecution was unable to prove prior hostility between the two gangs, stating at paragraph 34:

> *"Gangs will not necessarily commit their specific feuds to writing or to camera and declare their intent to seek revenge in a way that can be proved directly; that does not mean evidence of a gang's culture, membership and attitude towards violence will be irrelevant. It may provide an important link or part of an important link between an accused and the crime."*

It is worth noting that Lady Justice Hallett failed to address the concern that had been expressed by Lord Justice Lloyd-Jones in the earlier hearing when granting leave. At that stage he stated at paragraph 51 that it was:

> *"...arguable that the judge fell into error in his approach to this body of bad character evidence, and we are particularly concerned that there may have been a failure here to identify the precise purpose for which such evidence was to be admitted...it seems to us that it is at least arguable that there is an element of circularity about the way in which the prosecution proposed to use and did employ the evidence of bad character. In our view, it is arguable that such evidence could only become relevant for the purpose for which it seems to have been admitted if hostility between the two gangs was demonstrated."*

Lord Justice Lloyd-Jones' comments reflect the views of many practitioners who frequently argue that prosecution applications are too often made, circular in their logic and based on vague or unreliable evidence, such as drill lyrics and music. It would appear that counsel for the appellant in *Awoyemi* raised this point in his submissions. However, Lady Justice Hallett dismissed his concerns, stating at paragraph 32:

> *"...if applications to adduce evidence of gang membership by the Crown are becoming more common, this may be explained by the simple fact that so many offences are now gang related. It does not indicate that trial judges are too indulgent of the Crown. It is our experience that, as a general rule, trial judges are acutely conscious of the dangers of admitting gang affiliation evidence and take great care to ensure that bad character evidence is admitted through the appropriate gateway."*

Legal practitioners working in this area of law will have their own views on this response. Whatever the position though, the Court of Appeal very rarely reaches a conclusion on relevance that differs with the decision of the trial judge, even when dealing with inherently unreliable drill lyrics and videos.

CHAPTER SIX

LEWIS QUESTION 2: IS THERE PROPER EVIDENCE OF THE EXISTENCE AND NATURE OF THE GANG OR GANGS?

The criminal law in England and Wales traditionally takes a pragmatic approach to the admissibility of expert evidence. The lack of formal qualifications or credentials has never been determinative of whether an individual is entitled to give expert opinion evidence. Instead, as expressed by the Vice President of the Court of Appeal (Criminal Division) Lord Justice Fulford in *Byrne* [2021] EWCA Crim 107 at paragraph 99, the focus is whether the individual is "*competent to provide the Court with information likely to be outside the Court's own knowledge and experience, given [their] experience and professional background.*" In the context of gang evidence and drill lyrics, particularly when grappling with the second *Lewis* question, the criminal Courts have generally been content to allow the interpretation and contextualisation of such material to be given in form of police officers acting as gang experts.

Police officers as experts

The issue of police officers being relied upon as gang experts was dealt with by the Privy Council in *Myers* [2015] UKPC 40, the facts of which were set out in Chapter 5.

One of the issues for the Privy Council was whether a police officer's evidence on the nature of a gang ought to have been admitted. Having decided that the evidence was relevant to the issues in the case, the Privy Council confirmed that there was no rule against a police officer giving such evidence provided that the "*ordinary threshold requirements for expertise are established and providing that the ordinary rules as to the giving of expert evidence are observed*" (paragraph 57). The Privy Council observed that although different conditions may apply depending on the jurisdiction, essentially the police officer must:

> "*…make a sufficient study, whether by formal training or through practical experience, to assemble what can properly be regarded as a balanced body of specialised knowledge which would not be available to the tribunal of fact…. care must be taken that simple, and not necessarily balanced, anecdotal experience is not permitted to assume the robe of expertise.*" (paragraph 58)

The focus in *Myers* on a 'balanced body of specialised knowledge' essentially endorsed the approach adopted in England and Wales following the Court of Appeal decisions in *Edwards* [2001] EWCA Crim 2185 and *Hodges* [2003] EWCA Crim 290.

In *Edwards*, the appellant had been charged with supplying class A drugs after being found with a large amount of ecstasy tablets. He sought to call a drugs worker as an expert witness in support of his defence that the quantity of tablets was consistent with personal use. The prosecution in response sought to call a police officer to state the opposite, that the quantity was consistent with drugs supply. Both witnesses intended to give an opinion, based on what they had been told by drug users, on the consumption of drugs. The judge refused to allow either witness to give evidence. The Court of Appeal upheld the trial judge's decision stating that the evidence of both witnesses was "*classic hearsay*" and "*value-less*" given they had no medical or toxicological qualifications and their sources had not been identified (see paragraphs 12 to 14 of the judgment).

On one view the Court of Appeal decision in *Edwards* suggested that the established practice of police officers giving expert evidence may have been undermined. This was quickly dismissed by the Court of Appeal in *Hodges*, which confirmed that police officers were capable of being called to give expert evidence. The decision in *Edwards* was distinguished on the basis that the police officer in Hodges was experienced and his evidence, unlike in Edwards, did not trespass on areas of medical of scientific evidence. Furthermore, the Court of Appeal in *Hodges* cited with approval the judgment of Chief Justice King in the Australian Supreme Court in Bonython [1984] 38 SASR 45, to the effect that the "*body of knowledge or experience*" on which an expert's opinion is based must be "*sufficiently organised or recognised to be accepted as reliable body of knowledge or experience.*"

Rules and requirements for experts

The requirements set out in *Myers* are now largely codified in part 19 of the Criminal Procedure Rules 2020 ('CrPR') and Chapter 7 of the Criminal Practice Direction 2023 ('CPD'). They apply to all expert evidence, including police officer gang experts. Both the CrPR and CPD are comprehensive and are essential reading for practitioners tasked with considering expert evidence in this area.

Police officers put forward as experts are required to provide an opinion that is "*objective and unbiased*" and "*within the expert's area or areas of expertise*" (CrPR 19.2(a)).

The police officer is required to set out their qualifications, relevant experience and accreditation (CrPR 19.4(a)).

The police officer is required to state not only their conclusions but also how they arrived at them, in particular:

- If they are based on his own knowledge (CrPR 19.4(d))

- If they are based on information provided by some other person and, if so, identify that other person and the relevant information (CrPR 19.4(e))

Any witness statement or report produced by the police officer should identify any issues outside their area of expertise (19.2(3)(b).

The expectation is that the expert will produce a witness statement or report for proceedings which sets out the basis for their expertise, any information that "*might reasonably be thought capable of undermining the reliability of the expert's opinion, or detracting from the credibility or impartiality of the expert*" (CrPR 19.3(3)(c)(i)) and provide any party with an opportunity to inspect underlying material (CrPR 19.3(3(d)).

This is of particular significance when the police officer put forward as an expert has had some involvement in the investigation; the Court must be informed to assess what weight ought to be given to the evidence. As outlined in paragraph 60 of *Myers*:

> *"Compliance with these exacting standards can be difficult for a police officer who is effectively combining the duties of active investigator (if not of the current case) with those of independent expert. It is particularly important that such a witness should fully understand that once he is tendered as an expert he is not simply a part of the prosecution team but has a separate duty to the court to give independent evidence, whichever side it may favour. In particular a police expert needs to be especially conscious of the duty to state fully any material which weighs against any proposition which he is advancing, as well as all the evidence on which he has based that proposition. When considering an application by the Crown to adduce the evidence of a police expert, it is incumbent on the judge to satisfy himself that these duties are recognised, and discharged."*

Hearsay evidence and experts

As outlined above, the rules and requirements allow for the giving of expert opinion even if sourced from hearsay evidence. As the Privy Council acknowledged in paragraph 63 of the judgment in *Myers*:

> *"It is well established that an expert is entitled, in giving his evidence, to draw on the general body of knowledge and understanding in which he is expert, notwithstanding that some (or even all) of the material may have been assembled by other students of the subject."*

The Privy Council pointed to several authorities in various jurisdictions to emphasise the point, including *English Exporters (London) Ltd v Eldonwall Ltd* [1973] Ch 415. In that case, Mr Justice Megarry stated that an expert valuer was entitled to give an opinion on valuation which was based not only on his own personal experience of transactions but also from textbooks, journals, auction reports and exchanges with co-professionals (page 420). However, the fact that a witness may be an expert does not mean they will be immune from the restrictions on the admissibility of hearsay. For example, in *Eldonwall* Mr Justice Megarry refused to allow the valuer to give factual evidence about transactions in the case that he had no direct knowledge of himself. As stated at page 421 of his judgment:

> *"It is one thing to say 'From my general experience of recent transactions comparable with this one, I think the proper rent should be £x': it is another thing to say 'because I have been told by someone else that the premises next door have an area of x square feet and were recently let on such-and-such terms for £y a year, I say the rent of these premises should be £z a year'. What he has been told about the premises next door may be inaccurate or misleading as to the area, the rent, the terms and much else besides. It makes it no better when the witness expresses his confidence in the reliability of his source of information: a transparently honest and careful witness cannot make information reliable if, instead of speaking of what he has seen and heard for himself, he is merely retailing what others have told him."*

The Privy Council in Myers reached a similar view, stating at paragraph 66:

> *"The test of whether evidence based on hearsay material can be given is better seen to be whether it ceases to be the expounding of general*

> *study (whether by the witness or others) and becomes the assertion of a particular fact in issue in the case. The first is expert evidence, grounded on a body of learning or study; the second is not, even if it may be given by someone who is also an expert. The line between the two is case-specific, but it will usually be possible to discern it."*

In *Myers*, the police officer's evidence on the existence and nature of the gang was largely based on either his own observations in the local area or accumulated information collected by his unit. The Privy Council decided that such evidence was admissible as the body of knowledge for which he was an expert. However, if the police officer's evidence had been that an individual was a member of a gang based on particular sightings or if there had been a trigger event before the incident, it my "*pass the point at which it was no longer a matter of general study or accumulated knowledge, but required proof according to the ordinary rules*" (paragraph 67). The Privy Council stated that the evidential foundation must be clear and that the "*defence must not be left to explore what the sources were in speculative cross-examination before the jury*" (paragraph 70).

The point was repeated in the context of drill music in the recent case of *Dixon-Kenton* [2021] EWCA Crim 673. The appellant in that case was convicted of murder following a trial where the judge permitted the prosecution to present gang evidence in the form of drill YouTube videos. Although the Court of Appeal decided that the conviction was not rendered unsafe by the judge allowing the prosecution to adduce the gang evidence, the following warning was included at paragraph 33 of the judgment:

> *"Disagreements may arise when an expert moves from the general and contextual to the particular. It does not follow from PC Barr's undoubted expertise in Lambeth gangs that he was entitled to assert, without more, that X or Y was a member of a particular (or any) gang. That opinion would have to be based on admissible evidence which could be tested in the usual way and which also satisfied the requirements of the CJA."*

Although experts, including police gang officers, are entitled to draw on secondary sources or accumulated knowledge when giving evidence, the caselaw confirms that they are still bound by the hearsay rules.

Challenging police gang experts

Legal practitioners working in this area frequently criticise prosecution overreliance on police officers as gang experts. The work of the gang expert is often self-serving and based on law enforcement focused research. For example, police officers often rely on their experience of watching many drill music videos online to support their expertise. However, when taken through their actual experience, the police officer is often forced to concede that they have only watched videos made by people that they already suspected as gang members and it simply confirmed their suspicions. The police officers are often unable to point to any research by either them or their colleagues into the possibility that drill lyrics and videos may be a form of fiction.

So the inevitable question should be 'where is the 'balanced body of specialised knowledge' required in *Myers* and the CrPR?' Legal practitioners should subject this material to the scrutiny that was envisaged when the CrPR and CPD were introduced in relation to expert evidence. Unfortunately, having carefully reviewed the Court of Appeal authorities, it appears as though legal practitioners are too often prepared to accept the expertise of the gang officers.

In the case of *Awoyemi* [2016] EWCA Crim 668, the facts of which were set out in Chapter 5, counsel for one of the appellants sought to challenge the expertise of the police gang expert. However, he was told by the Court of Appeal that the expertise of the police officer had been accepted by trial counsel and therefore it was "*far too late to take the point now*" (paragraph 24). A similar observation was made by the Court of Appeal at paragraph 36 of the judgment in *Rashid* [2019] EWCA Crim 2018 where it was noted that "*no point was taken*" by the defence to the expertise of the police gang expert. For an example of the Court of Appeal criticising the "*inexcusably casual*" approach taken by the parties to expert evidence and the requirements under the CrPR, legal practitioners should read with care the case of *Berberi* [2014] EWCA Crim 2961.

The comments of the Court of Appeal suggest a failure by legal practitioners to both understand the relevant CrPR and effectively challenge the expertise of these witnesses who, as outlined elsewhere in this book, are tasked with giving evidence about highly controversial and contested areas of cultural practice. There is a real danger that gang experts are too often being given a free pass to give so called expert opinion even though it may be based upon unbalanced or unreliable source material. For example, in *Fender* [2018] EWCA Crim 2829, the Court of Appeal found that the police officer witness had sufficient expertise to comment on gangs partly because he had reviewed the gang matrix. As discussed in a Chapter 2, the gang matrix was not only criticised for racial profiling but also found to be unreliable; it was for that reason that the Metropolitan Police discontinued it in February 2024. It is not clear from the judgment in *Fender* whether the Court of Appeal was addressed on that highly criticised matrix but the judgment demonstrates the importance of legal practitioners undertaking careful scrutiny of the material that forms the basis for the apparent expertise.

Legal practitioners tasked with assessing the expertise of so called gang experts may find assistance from an unlikely source, namely the Court of Appeal judgment in *Brecani* [2021] EWCA Crim 731. The decision effectively neutered the National Referral Mechanism by ruling that decisions of caseworkers at the Single Competent Authority could not be admissible in criminal trials as they are not experts in human trafficking or modern slavery. However, in reaching that decision, the Court of Appeal stated at paragraph 54:

> "*It is not sufficient to assume that because administrators are likely to gain experience in the type of decision-making they routinely undertake that, simply by virtue of that fact, they can be treated as experts in criminal proceedings*"

Legal practitioners will find in a significant number of cases that so called gang experts have very little experience beyond routinely checking online drill lyrics and videos, looking for evidence that confirms pre-existing views. It may be arguable that those police officers, as was the case with Single Competent Authority caseworkers, do not have the requisite expertise and their opinions cannot be said to be based on a 'balanced body of specialised knowledge' as required in *Myers*.

CHAPTER SEVEN

LEWIS QUESTION 3: DOES THE EVIDENCE, IF ACCEPTED, GO TO SHOW THE DEFENDANT WAS A MEMBER OF OR ASSOCIATED WITH A GANG OR GANGS WHICH EXHIBITED VIOLENCE OR HOSTILITY TO THE POLICE OR WITH LINKS WITH FIREARMS?

Having established the existence and nature of the gang, the third step is to consider whether there is evidence showing the defendant's membership or affiliation to that gang. Is the prosecution able to demonstrate that the defendant has signed up to the culture and activities of the gang? Sometimes this is shown through police intelligence or records of arrest. However, legal practitioners working in this area know that most of the alleged gang material tends to be sourced from social media platforms, particularly in relation to rap and drill music.

Rap and drill music as evidence of gang association / membership

As outlined elsewhere in this book, the prosecution's reliance upon rap and drill music is controversial. It represents a distinctive brand of cultural expression and does not exist in a vacuum. It is almost exclusively used against disenfranchised young men living in deprived areas. It leans into stereotypes that those from the black community tend to be criminals. In the context of the third question in *Lewis* [2014] EWCA Crim 48, experience shows that the Court of Appeal has generally been content to find gang membership in most cases when presented with drill lyrics and videos featuring defendants, even where there is only a generic reference to guns and violence without any connection to the alleged offence.

In *Lewis*, Sir Brian Leveson acknowledged that there are evidential hurdles when attempting to prove an individual's membership or association with a gang, stating at paragraph 96 of the judgement that "*membership cards or documentary records of membership of street gangs were unlikely.*" The prosecution in that case had principally relied upon appearances by the appellants in several music videos that referenced gang activity. The point was made, and this continues to be frequently advanced in prosecution applications, that the presence of the appellants in the gang videos proved their membership as they would not have been permitted to be present unless trusted by the other gang members. Although the trial judge to his credit stated that something more than an appearance in a video would be necessary, Sir Brian Leveson took the broader view that even the appearance in a single video could show gang membership and association "*in appropriate circumstances*" (paragraph 99). In *Lewis* he dismissed the appellants' submissions that the videos showed nothing more than an involvement in that music genre, concluding that they were capable of showing membership or association with a gang or gangs exhibiting violence or hostility to the police or links with firearms.

Initial reluctance to find gang membership / association in *Alimi*

One of the first decisions of the Court of Appeal after *Lewis* suggested that a restrictive approach with a high bar would be applied in relation to the question of gang membership and association.

In *Alimi* [2014] EWCA Crim 2412, the appellant sought to appeal his convictions for firearm offences arising out of an incident in which he was accused with two others of discharging a firearm towards the police. At the start of the trial for the three defendants, the prosecution made a bad character application that included rap videos in which all three appeared. The lyrics were said to contain references to violence, guns and gang activity. However, only the two co-defendants spoke in the videos and the appellant's role was limited to appearing in the background. The judge allowed the videos to go before the jury as evidence against all three defendants, including the appellant.

Counsel for the appellant argued that although there was no question that the videos were admissible against the two co-defendants, they should not have been admitted against the appellant and the jury should have been directed to disregard them against him. The Court of Appeal agreed having summarised the points made by counsel:

> "*[Counsel] points out that there is no evidence that the lyrics or the music were apparent at the time when the videos were shot, as opposed to being dubbed in later. The appellant does not speak in the videos. He does not make any gang sign or wear any gang insignia or clothing. She points out that the appellant was simply appearing in the videos as an extra in a rap video film made on an estate in the area where the appellant grew up. The speakers in the rap lyrics were his friends. The fact that he was friends with [the co-defendants] is not evidence that he was implicated in gang activities with those other two men. [The co-defendants] have made reference to shooting, guns, ammunition and violence in those rap lyrics. The appellant does not.*"

Following a commendably rigorous review of the rap lyrics and videos, the Court of Appeal found that the third *Lewis* question had been satisfied in relation to the two co-defendants but not in relation to the appellant. The convictions were held to be unsafe and quashed. As will be clear by the end of this chapter, this was unfortunately an anomaly and every other decision of the Court of Appeal has typically adopted a broader approach to the question of evidence proving gang association and membership.

Expansive approach to the question of gang association / membership

In *Lewis*, Sir Brian Leveson had cited with approval the earlier case of *Elliott* [2010] EWCA Crim 2378, in which it was stated at paragraph 31:

> *"Violent gangs which provide no social amenity and exist for criminal purposes, are unlikely to issue membership cards, and so proof of membership will almost inevitably involve the prosecution putting forward evidence of a number of circumstances from which gang membership could be inferred."*

In *Elliott* the Court of Appeal was tasked with reviewing several different categories of evidence presented by the prosecution as allegedly showing gang association or membership. The evidence included images found on the appellant's mobile telephone in which he was shown making a sign with his hand shaped like a gun, making a 'P' sign, said to be the symbol of the PYG gang, with his hand and with a second individual wearing a black and white bandana. In a strikingly broader approach than that adopted in *Alimi*, the Court of Appeal upheld the convictions stating at paragraph 22 "*the fact that the appellant chose to be photographed striking such a pose in the company of a young man so dressed*" was capable of showing his membership or association with the gang.

Legal practitioners working in this area will be familiar with the Court of Appeal decision in *Awoyemi* [2016] EWCA Crim 668. The appellants in that case were alleged to have been members of the DAG gang who had attempted to shoot a rival gang member. The evidence of gang membership included:

- Handwritten rap lyrics found in one of the appellant's bedrooms referring to violence, drugs, guns and the DAG gang.

- YouTube music videos showing two of the appellants making gun gestures with their hands and rapping "*don't fuck with my family. Why? Cos I'll be eager to let slug fly*".

- Letters to and from one of the appellants referring to other gang members, gang related activity and endorsement of the DAG gang culture including retribution for the murder of members.

- Photographs on an appellant's phone showing a fellow gang member who had been the victim of a murder.

The Court of Appeal had no reluctance in concluding that the evidence demonstrated that each appellant was a member of the DAG gang. Adopting a literal reading of the material, the then Vice President of the Court of Appeal (Criminal Division) Lady Justice Hallett stated at paragraph 33:

> *"In each case, the gang affiliation evidence provided a link between them and a gang that gloried in violence and the use of firearms, mourned murdered friends and threatened violent retribution for those who crossed them...It went far beyond simple membership of a gang, the love of RAP music, hyperbole or appearance on a video. It indicated the extent to which the individuals concerned had signed up to gang and gun culture."*

The Court of Appeal adopted a particularly expansive approach in the cases of *Rashid* [2019] EWCA Crim 2018 and *Dixon-Kenton* [2021] EWCA Crim 673.

In *Rashid* [2019] EWCA Crim 2018, the appellants were convicted of various offences which included conspiracy to possess a firearm with intent to endanger life. Before opening the case, the prosecution applied for leave to adduce evidence in relation to gang membership, which included a drill music video titled "*Only time will tell*". All the appellants appeared in the video. The lyrics referred to the killing of a 14 year old boy called Corey Davis Junior in terms that made it clear that those participating in the video were celebrating the shooting that led to his death. Adopting a broad approach, the Court of Appeal upheld the trial judge's decision to admit the video as evidence against all the appellants, stating at paragraph 58 of the judgment:

> *"...it would not have been admissible but for the fact that the conspiracy related to guns. However, it was. As such, it was material because it showed [appellant], not involved in the shooting of Corey Davis Junior, but in a video exhorting that shooting."*

In *Dixon-Kenton* [2021] EWCA Crim 673, the 17 year old appellant had been convicted of murder following a trial where the judge permitted the prosecution to adduce gang evidence. The prosecution's case was that the appellant was a member of the Roupell Park (RP) gang and that the victim was a member of a rival gang. The evidence of alleged gang association included a YouTube music video called *Bling*. The video depicted several locations including the entrance to the Roupell Park estate. The appellant was shown in the video standing next to another person pointing to the '*Roupell Park*' sign, making an 'RP' hand sign himself and making derogatory gestures towards a sign for the rival gang's area. Adopting an expansive approach to the question, the Court of Appeal found that the video was "*relevant and probative of gang membership of the participants in the video*", that the appellant was participating in "*collective gang activity*" and that the "*impression given by his participation in the video is that the appellant was part of the gang*" (paragraph 51). Accordingly the appeal was refused and the judge's decision to admit the evidence was upheld.

Conclusion

The use of rap and drill music to establish alleged gang membership or association is controversial. There are legitimate concerns that it criminalises young people who simply have an interest in gang themed music because they find it fun, it helps them to appear more authentic in the industry, its boosts publicity in their music, or it is simply a nod to the local audience.

The categorisation of an individual as belonging to a gang should not be an easy decision for the Court. Experience teaches those of us who work with boys and young men that association and membership of streets gangs is fluid and often temporary. Legal practitioners tasked with representing actual gang members find it extremely difficult to establish a clear and direct link between them and the gang. Nevertheless, and despite the promise of the high bar adopted in the case of *Alimi*, the Court of Appeal has adopted a very broad approach to the third *Lewis* question. Unfortunately it seems as though anything more than a very minor or supporting role in rap and drill music videos will be enough for the prosecution to get the evidence before a jury.

CHAPTER EIGHT

LEWIS QUESTION 4: IF THE EVIDENCE IS ADMITTED, WILL IT HAVE SUCH AN ADVERSE EFFECT ON THE FAIRNESS OF THE PROCEEDINGS THAT IT OUGHT TO BE EXCLUDED?

The admissibility of gang evidence is not governed only by its relevance (*Lewis* Q1), support for the nature and existence of the gang (*Lewis* Q2) and proof of association and membership by the defendant (*Lewis* Q3). The fourth and final step requires a careful balancing exercise to be undertaken to determine the fairness of admitting the evidence under s.101(3) CJA 2003 and/or s.78 PACE 1978 i.e. does the probative value of the evidence outweigh the prejudicial effect of admitting it.

Legal practitioners working in this area know that gang evidence inevitably carries a high risk of unfair prejudice, particularly so in cases where the prosecution seek to rely on drill lyrics and videos. As outlined elsewhere in this book, drill lyrics and videos raise acute issues of fairness given the inevitable blurring of the lines between artistic expression, cultural identity and criminal conduct.

The fourth *Lewis* question requires the Court to assess whether the potential risk of admitting such evidence is so great that it should be excluded despite its potential relevance and probative value. As set out by the Privy Council in *Myers* [2015] UKPC 40 at paragraph 72:

> *"...it is necessary for the judge in every case to look carefully at the overall effect of gang evidence and to reach a judgment as to the balance*

> *between legitimate probative value and unfair prejudicial effect. When assessing that balance, a highly relevant consideration is the ability of the defendant to test the evidence. It is likely to be unfair for the witness to state a bald conclusion such as "I consider X to be a member of the M gang". The defence cannot be expected to embark upon speculative cross-examination as to the basis for such a conclusion, at the risk of inadvertently eliciting either inadmissible or unfair information."*

Approach to the question of fairness

The question of fairness tends to be the primary focus of most practitioners tasked with responding to prosecution applications to admit gang evidence. Indeed that was the position in *Lewis* [2014] EWCA Crim 48. The appellants focused their submissions on the insufficient probative value of the material as against the overwhelming prejudicial effect of it on the jury. The Court of Appeal ultimately found that the trial judge had fairly admitted the evidence and that it was for the jury to decide upon the appropriate weight to attach to it. That has been the general approach of the judiciary to the fourth *Lewis* question.

In *Saleem* [2007] EWCA Crim 1923 the appellant had sought to challenge the trial judge's decision to allow the prosecution to adduce rap lyrics referring to violence drafted at least 10 days before a violent assault. In a promising start to the judgment, Lord Justice Thomas acknowledged that the judge had not provided the jury with sufficient assistance in assessing both the relevance and the limitations of the rap lyrics. However, the conviction was not found to be unsafe because "*the jury would have appreciated the relevance of the evidence*" (paragraph 50) and there was other compelling evidence. The question should therefore be asked, if there was other compelling evidence against the appellant, was it fair for the judge at first instance to have allowed the prosecution to introduce highly prejudicial rap lyrics with limited probative value given the wider context of the evidence? The Court of Appeal expressed no concerns about the judge's decision on admissibility.

Another more recent decision is that of the Court of Appeal in *Soloman* [2019] EWCA Crim 1356. The appellant sought to appeal several convictions, which included possessing a firearm and ammunition with intent to endanger life. The prosecution case against him was that he had handed a bag containing a loaded firearm over to a third party knowing that it would be used for criminal purposes, and that he had intended to for it to be used to endanger life. During the trial, the judge had allowed the prosecution to present evidence of a note found on the appellant's mobile telephone. The note, which it was agreed had been created two days before the incident, appeared to be lyrics for a rap song titled "*sold guns to str8 killers*".

The Court of Appeal upheld the judge's decision that the rap lyrics were relevant to the issue of intent despite acknowledging at paragraph 12 of their judgment that:

> *"...the lyric seems to us of little weight in the context of this case, for the obvious reason that it appears to have been just that – a lyric – and that the lyrics of songs that people choose to record on their phones will often or perhaps typically have no connection to the factual reality of their own lives. That was a point which in our view, obvious as it might be, was one that it was necessary and appropriate for the judge to remind the jury of, either in his written directions or in his summing-up."*

Legal practitioners may find this decision difficult to square with the fourth *Lewis* question. The Court of Appeal agreed that the rap lyric had little probative weight or value in the case. The significant prejudicial effect of allowing the prosecution to adduce evidence which included the terms 'sold guns' to 'killers' in the context of the appellant's case was obvious. Yet there was no criticism of the decision to admit the evidence. Instead the focus was placed on the importance of judicial legal directions for the jury. However, in *Soloman*, the Court of Appeal was forced to acknowledge that the trial judge's directions had failed to assist the jury with both the relevance and limitations of the lyrics. Nevertheless, the convictions were not found to be unsafe for the same reasons identified in *Saleem* above:

> "*...it would have been apparent to the jury that the title of a lyric found on the appellant's phone could not be given much weight or significance and it would have been reasonably apparent to the jury that lyrics of a song do not necessarily or perhaps commonly bear a connection with actual real life events. Furthermore, there was other, much more weighty evidence upon which the prosecution relied which we have mentioned earlier in this judgment which provided compelling proof of the appellant's guilt. This lyric was of marginal significance in the case.*" (paragraph 15)

The Court of Appeal reasoning in both *Saleem* and *Soloman* is consistent with much of the gang evidence caselaw. They will very rarely interfere with a trial judge's decision to admit material on fairness grounds. The focus instead will be on the suitability of the legal directions as "*it is for the jury to decide whether the contentions based on the gang-related evidence were established*" (paragraph 51 of *Heslop* [2022] EWCA Crim 897).

Focus on fairness and legal directions

The Court typically expresses little concern for how gang evidence, particularly in the form of rap and drill music, might unduly prejudice a jury against the defendant. As was endorsed in cases such *Heslop* and *O* [2010] EWCA Crim 2985, it is for the jury to decide whether the relevant evidence is "*part of art or part of life*" (paragraph 24 of *O*). However, there is no formal requirement upon the trial judge to explain to the jury the important cultural context and artistic influences inherent within rap and drill music. Is it possible that we underestimate the prejudicial effect such lyrics have on jurors? Do we overestimate the ability of ordinary members of the public to put aside natural bias and avoid a literal interpretation of such evidence? It is possible that juries frequently attach greater value to the content of drill and rap music than is justified?

For that reason legal practitioners must continue to persevere with objections to the admission of gang evidence on the grounds of fairness. The focus ought to be on demonstrating the limited probative value of the material in light of the significant prejudicial effect. Is the material only tenuously connected to the alleged offence? What is the age of the gang evidence? Is the material filled with descriptions of gratuitous violence, graphic details or provocative language? Will the evidence have an emotional effect on the jury? Will the defence be able to properly challenge the content of the material? Will the admission of the gang evidence result in an increase in the complexity and length of the trial, particularly where it is multi-handed? Whatever the decision made in relation to relevance, nature/existence of the gang and a defendant's association/membership of it, the fourth Lewis question demands careful consideration by the Court. Ultimately the trial must remain fair.

If, as is often the case with prosecution applications to admit gang evidence, the judge rules that at least some of the gang evidence will go before the jury, legal practitioners must be ready to suggest comprehensive legal directions for the judge. To assist in this process, those who defend ought to have adduced some evidence, preferably in the form of a defence expert, addressing the culture and artistic elements of rap and drill music. To ensure fairness, the judge must be invited to adopt legal directions that include the following:

- A summary of both the prosecution and defence submissions on the potential relevance of the evidence to the issue in the case.

- A warning that the jury must be sure that the defendant was either associated with or a member of the identified gang before any use can be made of the evidence.

- A reminder that mere association with or membership of a gang does not equate to guilt.

- Identification of the limitations inherent in the evidence, particularly where admitted in the form of drill lyrics and videos.

- A warning that the jury must avoid falling into the trap of 'guilt by association'.

- A warning that the jury must not convict a defendant on the strength of gang evidence alone.

PART 3

INJUNCTIONS AND ANCILLARY ORDERS

CHAPTER NINE

USING CIVIL INJUNCTIONS AND ORDERS TO CONTROL GANGS AND DRILL MUSIC

Over the past decade, both the police and prosecution have increasingly relied upon a hybrid selection of injunctions and orders to regulate the behaviour of those accused of involvement in gangs. These injunctions and orders undoubtedly amount to a blurring of the line between civil and criminal law. The two most controversial are gang injunction and criminal behaviour orders. Although they may have been introduced for purposes such as reducing anti-social behaviour, reducing violence among young people and discouraging gang activity, these civil enforcement tools are frequently utilised to police young black men and boys involved in local youth culture, particularly in the form of rap and drill music.

Gang Injunctions

Gang injunctions were introduced in the Policing and Crime Act 2009 following the creation of similar orders in the United States of America. The original aim was to reduce gang-related violence. The provisions allow both local authorities and the police to make applications in relation to individuals suspected of involvement in gangs, even where there is insufficient evidence to secure a criminal conviction. The injunctions often include prohibitions on associating with individuals, entering certain streets / boroughs, wearing certain clothing or colours and, significantly in the context of rap and drill lyrics, posting material online. As outlined in Chapter 10, the broad application of gang injunctions has led to criticism from legal practitioners working in this area, particularly on behalf of young black men and boys, who face significant difficulties opposing the imposition of these sweeping orders.

Criminal Behaviour Orders

Criminal behaviour orders were introduced in the Anti-Social Behaviour, Crime and Policing Act 2014, which replaced the frequently criticised anti-social behaviour orders. Unlike gang injunctions, the orders are only imposed following a criminal conviction. However, they are civil orders that extend the Court's ability to regulate the everyday life of those subject to them, typically young people. The conditions frequently attached to the orders include curfews, prohibitions on association, area exclusions but also restrictions on artistic and cultural production. Again these orders have been criticised for going too far, particularly by enforcing a level of social control unrelated to the original criminal case. See Chapter 11 below for the full analysis and discussion.

Policing Drill Music

It is in the area of rap and drill music that gang injunctions and criminal behaviour orders have attracted the most public attention. As outlined in earlier chapters of this book, drill music has become embedded within the lived experiences of many living within deprived inner city boroughs. It has become a lightning rod for debates about violence, race and gangs in Parliament, national media and local communities. The police and prosecution authorities frequently argue that drill lyrics and videos glorify violence, knife crime and gang wars. It is on this basis that gang injunctions and criminal behaviour orders have been used to restrict drill artists in the production of music, the release of drill tracks and performing music live. For example, legal practitioners working in this area will have experience of injunctions and orders requiring musicians to submit both their lyrics and videos to the police for review before they can be distributed.

For those who support the measures, such draconian interventions are justified on the basis that they address the risk that such music may encourage violence and create a danger to the public. For those opposed to these civil restrictions, the criticism is frequently made that they criminalise creativity and render important cultural expression as evidence of criminal activity rather than social commentary or art. Furthermore, it is frequently pointed out by legal practitioners in Court when opposing these measures that there is little to no evidence that suggests musical restrictions of this type reduce either serious youth violence or gang activities.

The story of gang injunction and criminal behaviour orders may well be one of legal innovation, smartly walking a fine line between criminal punishment and civil control, but with the consequence that it drives drill music underground and deepens the distrust that already exists between marginalised communities and those in positions of authority.

CHAPTER TEN

GANG INJUNCTIONS

A gang injunction is a civil tool that allows the police or a local authority to apply to the County Court, High Court or Youth Court for an injunction against an individual to prevent gang related violence and drug dealing. They are typically applied for where a criminal prosecution has either not been pursued by the Crown Prosecution Service or, where an individual has been charged, the case has not yet concluded or the individual has been acquitted at trial.

Gang injunctions were first introduced under Part 4 of the Policing and Crime Act 2009 ('PCA 2009') and subsequently amended by both the Crime and Security Act 2010 ('CSA 2010') and the Serious Crime Act 2015 ('SCA 2015'). The explicit aim of the legislation was to try and break down violent gang culture, prevent an escalation in violent gang behaviour and engage gang members in positive activities to help them walk away from the gangs.

The introduction of gang injunctions reflected a wider trend towards the use of civil preventative orders when dealing with alleged criminal behaviour in England and Wales. The measures blur the boundary between criminal law and civil law by enabling the Court to impose not only restrictions but positive requirements on individuals in the absence of a criminal conviction, while attaching punitive consequences for breach of the orders.

Legal practitioners working in this area are frequently tasked with responding to applications for gang injunctions that rely upon the client's interest and involvement in drill music. This has led to several high profile cases covered by the national media. For example, in January 2019, drill rap duo AM and Skengso were handed suspended prison sentences for breaching an interim gang injunction by performing a particular song at a concert that police argued had the potential to provoke violence. This has led to criticism that the orders are too often used to censor and punish particularly young black men and boys involved in the drill music scene and, arguably, infringe upon their rights protected under several articles of the European Convention on Human Rights ('ECHR').

Background to the introduction of Part 4 of the Policing and Crime Act 2009

Part 4 of the PCA 2009 was passed by Parliament in response to the Court of Appeal decision in *Birmingham City Council v Shafi* [2008] EWCA Civ 1186.

In *Shafi*, the local authority had sought a civil injunction under s.222 of the Local Government Act 1972. The individual was said to be a gang member. The local authority had sought an injunction preventing him from associating with certain named individuals in any public place and from entering large parts of the city of Birmingham; in short, a type of gang injunction which relied upon police intelligence rather than first hand evidence.

The judge at first instance had refused the local authority application stating that he had no jurisdiction to make an order but, even if he did, the criminal standard had not been satisfied for the imposition of such an order. The Court of Appeal held that although the judge did have jurisdiction to make such an order it was limited to "*exceptional cases*" and it would have been wrong in principle for the Court to exercise the discretion in that case; particular emphasis was placed on the importance of the Court not imposing injunctions without "*detailed checks and balances developed by Parliament*" (paragraph 60).

Parliament responded by introducing Part 4 of the PCA 2009, reversing the effect of the decision in *Shafi* and placing gang injunctions on a clear statutory footing.

Statutory framework

Under s.34(1) PCA 2009, the Court may grant an application for a gang injunction against any individual aged 14 years or older.

The application may only be made by the chief officer of police, the chief constable of the British Transport Police or the local authority (s.37 PCA 2009). The Crown Prosecution Service should typically be informed of any such application to ensure that it does not interfere with any parallel criminal investigation, bail conditions or ongoing proceedings.

Jurisdiction depends on the age of the individual; for those 18 years or older the application is heard in either the County Court or the High Court, for those aged 14 to 17 it is heard in the Youth Court.

The Court may only grant an application for a gang injunction if two conditions are met.

Under s.34(2) PCA 2009, the first condition is that the Court must be satisfied on the balance of probabilities that the individual has engaged in or has encouraged or assisted:

(a) Gang-related violence, or

(b) Gang-related drug-dealing activity

Under s.34(3) PCA 2009, the second condition is that the Court thinks it is necessary to grant the injunction for either or both of the following purposes:

(a) To prevent the individual from engaging in, or encouraging or assisting gang-related violence or gang-related drug-dealing activity

(b) To protect the individual from gang-related violence or gang-related drug-dealing activity.

Under s.34(5) PCA 2009, something is considered 'gang-related' if it "*occurs in the course of, or otherwise related to, the activities of a group*" that:

(a) Consists of at least three people, and

(b) Has one or more characteristics that enable its members to be identified as a group.

It is worth emphasising that the original version of s.34(5)(b) PCA 2009 required the group to be identifiable by name, emblem or colour and by association with a particular area. However, s.51 SCA 2015 removed those requirements on the basis that it had the effect of rendering the definition unduly restrictive. The point was made that many gangs and their members do not have a name, emblem or colour and, increasingly in recent years, gangs do not restrict their criminality to their own associated areas e.g. members travel all over the country as part of county lines operations. The result is a deliberately broader definition capable of capturing a wider range of individuals and activities.

The terms of a gang injunction may <u>prohibit</u> specified conduct. Under s.35(2) PCA 2009, individuals may be prohibited from:

(a) being in a particular place;

(b) being with particular persons in a particular place;

(c) being in charge of a particular species of animal in a particular place;

(d) wearing particular descriptions of articles of clothing in a particular place;

(e) using the internet to facilitate or encourage violence or drug-dealing activity.

The terms of a gang injunction may require specified conduct. Under s.35(3) PCA 2009, individuals may be required to:

(a) notify the person who applied for the injunction of the individual's address and of any change to that address;

(b) be at a particular place between particular times on particular days;

(c) present himself or herself to a particular person at a place where he or she is required to be between particular times on particular days;

(d) participate in particular activities between particular times on particular days.

Under s.35(5) PCA 2009, the prohibitions and requirements included in the injunction must, so far as is practicable, be such as to avoid:

(a) any conflict with the individual's religious beliefs, and

(b) any interference with the times, if any, at which the individual normally works or attends any educational establishment.

The legislation makes it explicitly clear that applications for gang injunctions should be based upon and supported by multi-agency partnership working. Before making the application, the police or local authority must comply with specific consultation requirements as set out in s.38(2) PCA 2009. The applicant is required to consult any relevant local authority, chief police officer and other body or individual that is thought appropriate. Where relevant the Court typically expects the applicant to have either consulted or explained why they have not consulted the local probation service, local children's services, headteacher / principal of the individual's school or college and the individual's housing providers. Legal practitioners must remember that where the individual is aged between 14 and 17, the applicant is required to consult with the relevant Youth Offending Team and the Court will have expected some engagement with the young person's parents / family. The application for a gang injunction is unlikely to be successful without the input of these other agencies and individuals. Legal practitioners responding to such applications must request disclosure of the steps that have been taken to engage in this consultation.

Under s.36(2) PCA 2009, the terms of a gang injunction must not exceed 2 years beginning on the day in which the injunction was made by the Court.

The breach of a gang injunction is not a criminal offence. For adults it is dealt with as a civil contempt of court in either the County Court or High Court, which is punishable by up to two years in prison and/or an unlimited fine (s.14(4A) of the Contempt of Court Act 1981). For those aged 14 to 17, a separate statutory scheme allows the Youth Court to impose either a supervision order or a detention order (schedule 5A of the Crime and Security Act 2010). Before making either a supervision order or a detention order the Youth Court must obtain and consider a report prepared by the Youth Offending Team.

Appeals may be lodged by either party following the grant, refusal, variation or discharge of a gang injunction. For adults, appeals against decisions of either the County Court or the High Court are governed by part 52 of the Civil Procedure Rules. Under s.46B of the PCA 2009, individuals aged 14 to 17 have a statutory right of appeal to the Crown Court against a decision made by the Youth Court. Applications for permission to appeal must normally be filed within 21 days of the Court decision.

Burden and standard of proof

As outlined above, under s.34(2) PCA 2009 the burden of proving that an individual has engaged in either gang-related violence or gang-related drug-dealing activity falls on the applicant i.e. the police or local authority. The standard of proof is expressly stated to be the civil standard i.e. the balance of probabilities.

Nevertheless, in *Birmingham City Council v Jones* [2023] UKSC 27, the Supreme Court was asked to consider whether the right to a fair hearing under article 6(1) of the ECHR required the application of the criminal standard of proof in such cases given the potentially significant effect upon the individual's right to respect for his family life, private life, and home as well as his rights to freedom of association and expression.

The Supreme Court considered the general approach of the European Court of Human Rights in these types of cases, noting at paragraph 31 of the judgment that it had "*shown itself reluctant to rule on particular rules of evidence in isolation and is more concerned to assess whether the national proceedings considered as a whole were fair as required by article 6(1).*" Specific reference was made to the authorities of *Garcia Ruiz v Spain* (1999) 31 EHRR 22, *Dombo Beheer BV v The Netherl*ands (1993) 18 EHRR 213 and *Saliba v Malta* (Application 24221/13) (unreported).

In *Saliba*, civil proceedings were brought alleging that the appellant had committed a robbery. The national Court applied the civil standard of proof, namely the balance of probabilities, and held the appellant liable. He subsequently brought proceedings before the Strasbourg Court alleging infringement of his rights under article 6(1), particularly alleging that the national Court had failed to apply an adequate standard of proof. The Strasbourg Court held that while article 6 guarantees the right to a fair hearing, it "*does not lay down any rules on the admissibility of evidence or the way it should be assessed, which are primarily matters for regulation by national law and national courts*" (paragraph 63). It was accepted that article 6(1) required the tribunal to undertake "*a proper examination of the submissions, arguments and evidence adduced by the parties*" and that "*the right to a fair trial cannot be seen as effective unless the requests and observations of the parties are truly heard, that is to say, properly examined by the tribunal*" (paragraphs 64 and 65). However, when grappling with the distinction between civil and criminal cases, the Strasbourg Court concluded at paragraph 67 that:

> "*...the requirements inherent in the concept of "fair hearing" are not necessarily the same in cases concerning the determination of civil rights and obligations as they are in cases concerning the determination of a criminal charge. This is borne out by the absence of detailed provisions such as paragraphs 2 and 3 of Article 6 applying to cases of the former category. Thus, although these provisions have a certain relevance outside the strict confines of criminal law, the Contracting States have greater latitude when dealing with civil cases concerning civil rights and obligations than they have when dealing with criminal cases.*"

In short, the Strasbourg Court in *Saliba* determined the case without making any criticism of the national Court's application of the civil standard of proof. Instead, as observed by the Supreme Court in *Jones*, emphasis was placed on principles such as the equality of arms, affording the parties a fair opportunity to present their cases, giving reasons for decisions etc. The Supreme Court noted that Part 4 of the PCA 2009 included procedural safeguards, such as the 2 year limit for the imposition of gang injunctions and the consultation requirement, which ensured the fairness of the overall proceedings.

The Supreme Court in *Jones* concluded its consideration of the issue by stating at paragraph 38:

> "*It is clear, therefore, that the Strasbourg authorities to which we have been referred provide no support for the view that a fair hearing under article 6(1) requires the application of the criminal standard of proof in circumstances such as those in the present appeal. While it would be open to the Strasbourg Court to develop its jurisprudence on article 6(1) so as to require the application of the criminal standard of proof in such circumstances, there is no sign in its case law to date that such a development is likely*".

Accordingly, legal practitioners working in this area should not waste much time drafting lengthy legal arguments about the compatibility of the standard of proof under s.34 PCA 2009 with article 6 of the ECHR.

Presentation of evidence

The presentation of the evidence in support of the application for a gang injunction is entirely a matter for the applicant. It is often served in the form of a draft gang injunction along with a supporting statement and exhibits. Legal practitioners must carefully consider the material and determine whether it is relevant to the application and therefore admissible.

The Home Office Practitioner's Guide '*Gang-Related Violence and Gang-Related Drug Dealing*' is a very useful resource for those working in this area. When considering the relevance of any evidence, legal practitioners ought to have regard to paragraph 2.1.2 of the guide which makes it clear that the alleged violence and/or drug dealing:

> "*...must be associated with the activities of a group. This will require the applicant authority to prove what the group does. This will normally be some form of unlawful activity – drug distribution, money laundering, car theft, identity theft, or multiple forms of criminality, all supported by violence or the threat of violence.*"

The starting point for the Court is often to consider all the evidence presented by the applicant and consider submissions about the weight that ought to be attached to it. The material is frequently in the form of direct evidence from witnesses, hearsay evidence from police officers and members of the community, documentary evidence, expert evidence, CCTV / video evidence, details of previous arrests / convictions and, significantly in the context of young individuals involved in drill music, material obtained from social media accounts.

Legal practitioners ought to be prepared to challenge the relevance of the material, particularly where it has little probative value to alleged gang-related violence and / or drug dealing. Furthermore, those representing the individuals subject to these applications ought to be prepared to obtain and serve their own evidence. For example, legal practitioners should consider instructing child psychologists to assess their young clients with the particular focus of any report being the ability of their young client to understand and comply with the proposed terms of the gang injunction.

Necessity and proportionality

The terms of most proposed gang injunctions inevitably impact on the individual's rights under the ECHR. As outlined above, the terms frequently engage the right to private and family life (article 8), freedom of expression (article 10) and freedom of association (article 11). Consequently, applicants must ensure that any infringement is both necessary and proportionate.

The issue was considered by the Court of Appeal in *Murray v Chief Constable of Lancashire Constabulary* [2015] EWCA Civ 1174. The appellant sought to appeal the refusal of the judge at first instance to either discharge or vary an interim gang injunction. The police had applied for interim injunctions against the appellant and six other members of the same gang. The evidence sought to demonstrate that the appellant and other members of his gang were involved in the illegal drugs trade, using firearms and weapons to control and intimidate rivals. The appellant denied involvement. Nevertheless the interim gang injunction was made and there was a later refusal to either discharge it entirely or vary the terms at the request of the appellant.

The appellant argued that the judge below had erred as the terms of the injunction sought to address gang behaviour outside the range of specific activities alleged against him; in other words, he was being held responsible for the activities of the wider gang despite there being no evidence of his personal involvement. In dismissing the appeal, Lord Justice McCombe stated that the judge had been entitled to consider the wider activities of the gang. He stated at paragraph 24:

> "*It seems to me that the violence attributed to the gangs in this case could scarcely have been more serious. It appears to have been a matter of serendipity which gang member committed or participated in which gang action. There was good evidence that may in the end establish that the respondents were, to use a well-worn phrase, 'in it together' in the operation of the gang's activities.*"

Legal practitioners must approach the above passage with care. It is often cited by eager applicants as justification for the Court taking a broad brush approach to the specific terms included within the draft gang injunction. In those situations, the Court ought to be taken to the comments made by Lord Justice McCombe later in the judgment on the requirements of necessity and proportionality:

> "*29. However, once the "threshold" for the grant of an interim injunction is crossed, obviously, the judge cannot simply impose, or continue unthinkingly, any injunction, without careful consideration of whether the orders applied for "fit the bill". He must apply his mind conscientiously to the statutory question of whether the precise injunctions are suitable in the particular case, having regard to the ultimate question of whether or not they will be shown to be "necessary" when the case reaches its final hearing. The orders must not be punitive and must be confined by the relevant necessity in the case of each respondent…*
>
> *30. The judge must obviously also consider the proportionality of the individual orders sought and must not be tempted to act merely upon a police "template" of types of order sought and/or granted in other cases – a trend that is sometimes apparent, for example, in the Criminal Division of this court in relation to Sexual Offences Prevention Orders made under the Sexual Offences Act 2003 . Equally, he must have*

regard to the length of time that the orders may be in place before the final hearing."

The principles as explained by Lord Justice McCombe in *Murray* are reflected within paragraph 7.2 of the Home Office Practitioner's Guide '*Gang-Related Violence and Gang-Related Drug-Dealing*', specifically where it states that the "*applicant authority will need to ensure that the infringement is necessary, justified and proportionate, which generally means tailoring the restriction as narrowly as possible.*"

Legal practitioners tasked with responding to applications for gang injunctions must have the principles of necessity and proportionality at the forefront of their submissions when addressing the terms of any proposed order. This is particularly important in cases where the applicant has sought to place restrictions on an individual's access to social media and engagement with others. Experience shows that such restrictions stifle those interested in and involved with culturally significant activities such as producing drill music; the message is frequently sent to those individuals, often already socially marginalised young people, that their cultural activities are unacceptable and will be policed. Unfortunately, those of us working in this area know that the Court has very rarely proven receptive to these types of submissions.

Nevertheless, when considering the draft orders and supporting material, legal practitioners ought to be asking the following questions:

- Does the evidence show that the prohibitions or requirements are necessary to prevent gang-related violence or gang-related drug dealing?

- Does the evidence show that the prohibitions or requirements are necessary to protect the individual from gang-related violence or gang-related drug dealing?

- Are the prohibitions and requirements targeted at the needs and behaviour of the particular individual?

- Are the prohibitions and requirements enforceable?

- Are the prohibitions and requirements clear, concise and easy for the individual to understand?

- Do the prohibitions and requirements have any implications for the individuals' human rights, including those protected under the UN Convention on the Rights of the Child?

- Will the prohibitions and requirements have the effect of protecting and reassuring the public?

Legal practitioners should also highlight the statutory obligation on both local authorities and the police under s.11 of the Children Act 2004 to ensure in discharging their functions that they have regard to the need to safeguard and promote the welfare of children. The statutory safeguard is often useful when addressing the necessity and proportionality of the proposed injunction, particularly as the applicant is required to demonstrate that appropriate risk assessments have been undertaken. All proposed prohibitions and requirements must have been checked by the applicant to ensure that they would not compromise the safety of either the individual or others associated with the individual. For example, legal practitioners may be able to establish that an exclusion requirement would leave an individual not only isolated from his contemporary support network but exposed to danger from those outside his support network i.e. rival gang members.

Potential consequences of gang injunctions

As outlined in the introduction to this chapter, applications for gang injunctions have attracted significant attention and inevitable criticism in recent years. Legal practitioners tasked with responding to these applications require not only a complete understanding of the legislation and relevant case law, but also an appreciation of the real world impact of labelling boys and young men as gang members. This book has previously addressed the point that too often groups of young people, especially black boys and young men, are labelled as gang members when they are in fact part of a friendship group in which some individuals may engage in criminal behaviour.

Imposing a gang injunction upon young people has the obvious consequence of stigmatising them as gang members. Legal practitioners working in this area will have interacted with boys and young men who feel, whether rightly or wrongly, that they have been written off by society. They associate the police, almost always the applicant in these cases, as the enemy, which discourages any future engagement with them or other authority figures. Having been labelled as gang members by the Court, these boys and young men are put at increased risk from other young people associated with rival gangs. The final and most significant consequence of imposing these orders is that they are counterproductive and simply do not work; far from pulling individuals out, by labelling them as gang members the Court essentially glamourises their activities resulting in further and potentially more serious offending.

CHAPTER ELEVEN

CRIMINAL BEHAVIOUR ORDERS

A Criminal Behaviour Order ('CBO') is an order made for the purpose of preventing a defendant in criminal proceedings from engaging in behaviour that is likely to cause harassment, alarm or distress to another person in the future.

The terms of a CBO may prohibit a defendant from doing anything described in the order and/or require the defendant to do anything described in the order.

In recent years these orders have been used by the prosecution to attempt to disrupt alleged gang offending, which has included placing severe restrictions on those involved in the drill music scene.

Statutory framework

The CBO regime was introduced under the Anti-Social Behaviour, Crime and Policing Act 2014 but was subsequently consolidated into Part 11 of Chapter 1 of the Sentencing Act 2020 ('SA 2020') in December 2020. It replaced the previous anti-social behaviour order ('ASBO') provisions.

Under s.331 SA 2020, the Court will only consider making a CBO if the following pre-conditions are satisfied:

- The defendant has been convicted of a criminal offence. The type of offence is irrelevant to the application.

- The prosecution has made an application to the Court for a CBO to be made against the defendant. Notice of an intention to apply for the CBO must be served as soon as practicable in accordance with Criminal Procedure Rule 31.3.

- The CBO will be made in addition to dealing with the defendant for the criminal offence i.e. sentencing.

- The defendant has not been sentenced by way of an absolute discharge for the original criminal offence.

The CBO does not have to be made at the same time as the passing of sentence and may be adjourned to a later date (s.332(3) SA 2020). As applications for CBOs are frequently served shortly before the sentencing hearing, the Court tends to adjourn the decision to a later date to allow the prosecution to properly prepare the application and to afford the defence time to prepare a response. This was considered the most "*desirable*" approach by the Court of Appeal in *Rothwell* [2021] EWCA Crim 1047 where the prosecution had clearly been unprepared to deal with the application. However, the Court is required to have adjourned consideration of the CBO <u>before</u> passing sentence; if the defendant were sentenced and the prosecution subsequently decided some days or weeks later to make a CBO application, the Court would not be able to consider it.

The Court has the power to make an <u>interim CBO</u> if it thinks it is just to do so (s.335 SA 2020). An interim order can be made to run until either the final hearing or until making a further order. The Court often imposes an interim order when the decision has been made to adjourn consideration of the CBO application to a date after the sentencing hearing. When making an interim CBO the Court has the same powers as if making a final CBO.

The Court must consider <u>two conditions</u> before making a CBO under s.331(2) SA 2020.

Condition 1 – is the Court satisfied that the defendant engaged in behaviour that caused or was likely to cause harassment, alarm or distress to any person?

Condition 2 – does the Court consider that making the order will help in preventing the defendant from engaging in such behaviour?

The relevant law in relation to the application of the two conditions and the principles underlying the scope of the CBO terms is set out in detail below.

Before applying for a CBO for a defendant under 18 years old, the prosecution must obtain the views of the local Youth Offending Team (s.331(5) SA 2020).

Under s.334(1) SA 2020, any CBO made will take effect on the day that it is imposed by the Court unless the defendant is already subject to a separate CBO, in which case the new CBO may take effect on the day on which the previous CBO ends.

The CBO must state the length of the order. For defendants under 18 years old, the CBO must be made for no less than 1 year and no more than 3 years (s.334(4) SA 2020). For defendants 18 years or older, the CBO must be made for a minimum of 2 years or for an indefinite period i.e. until further order (s.334(5) SA 2020). It is worth noting that CBOs imposed for an indefinite period are rare and reserved for the most extreme cases.

Under s.336 SA 2020, either party may apply to subsequently vary or discharge the CBO. However, repeated defence applications after a refusal by the Court will require either the consent of the Court or agreement of the prosecution before being considered on a further occasion.

It is a criminal offence to breach the terms of a CBO (s.339 SA 2020). The maximum sentence on summary conviction is 6 months imprisonment and/or an unlimited fine. The maximum sentence on indictment is 5 years imprisonment and/or an unlimited fine.

A defendant has the right to appeal against the imposition of a CBO made by either the Magistrates' Court or the Youth Court under s.108 of the Magistrates' Court Act 1980 ('MCA 1980'); the provisions allow for an appeal against sentence which includes orders made on conviction. If a CBO is made by the Crown Court, the defendant's appeal will be to the Court of Appeal Criminal Division in accordance with s.9 of the Criminal Appeal Act 1968 ('CAA 1968').

Legal test and the two conditions

As previously outlined, the Court must consider two specific conditions before making a CBO under s.331 SA 2020:

Condition 1 – is the Court satisfied that the defendant engaged in behaviour that caused or was likely to cause harassment, alarm or distress to any person?

Condition 2 – does the Court consider that making the order will help in preventing the defendant from engaging in such behaviour?

The first condition requires the Court to be satisfied that the defendant has engaged in behaviour that caused or was likely to have caused harassment, alarm or distress to any person (s.331(1)(a).

Legal practitioners with experience of the ASBO regime will observe a significant difference in the wording of this condition compared with its predecessor. Parliament removed the ASBO requirement that the behaviour be directed towards a person 'not of the same household'.

The prosecution is not required to establish a link between the criminal behaviour that led to the defendant's conviction and the behaviour sought to be addressed by the CBO. Essentially any criminal proceedings resulting in a defendant's conviction can be used as a springboard to apply for a CBO. However, when making an application for a CBO that has no nexus to the conviction, the prosecution should address the reasons for making the order. If this is not done those representing the defendant ought to be challenging the basis for the application.

The burden will be on the prosecution to prove to the criminal standard i.e. beyond reasonable doubt, that the defendant engaged in behaviour that caused or was likely to have caused harassment, alarm or distress to a person. There are two steps for the Court. Firstly, has the prosecution made the Court sure that the defendant engaged in the behaviour alleged in the application? Secondly, has the prosecution made the Court sure that the defendant's behaviour caused or was likely to have caused harassment, alarm or distress to any person?

The prosecution can and almost always does rely upon the defendant's prior conduct, including non-conviction matters. But there is no restriction on the defendant presenting evidence of his own (s.332(1) SA 2020). The strict rules of evidence in criminal proceedings do not apply. It will not matter that the evidence sought to be relied upon would have been inadmissible in the criminal proceedings in which the defendant was convicted e.g. bad character, hearsay etc. This is because the proceedings are civil notwithstanding the fact that an application for a CBO will be heard at the conclusion of criminal proceedings in a criminal Court. Legal practitioners working in this area will know that the consequence of this relaxed approach to supporting evidence is that frequently the Court will consider and rely upon material obtained from the defendant's social media, such as drill lyrics and videos, which had perhaps previously been ruled inadmissible in the criminal proceedings.

The <u>second condition</u> is that the Court must consider that the making of the order would help in preventing the defendant from engaging in behaviour which would cause or would likely cause harassment, alarm or distress to any person (s.331(1)(b) SA 2020).

This second stage of the test is fundamentally different from the previous ASBO regime. The Court no longer must be satisfied that the order is 'necessary', only that it will be 'helpful'. Accordingly, the case law relating to 'necessity' under the previous ASBO regime is no longer relevant, which has inevitably resulted in a lowering of the legislative threshold for allowing CBO applications.

It is worth noting that applications for ASBOs frequently failed when the issue of necessity was considered by the Court. In *R (F) v Bolton Crown Court* [2009] EWHC 240 (Admin), the Administrative Court decided that an ASBO imposed on a youth was not necessary because he had been sentenced to a 2 year supervision order together with a curfew which provided adequate protection to those affected by his behaviour. Similarly in *R (Cooke) v DPP* [2008] EWHC (Admin), the Administrative Court found that an order was not necessary because the individual's mental health meant that he would be unable to comply with its terms; the Court stated at paragraph 12 that it would be *"a wrong exercise of the Court's discretion…to make an order in circumstances where the Court knows that the defendant is not capable of complying with it."*

Legal practitioners engaged in this work know that the updated definition has resulted in a significant watering down of the test. Previously those representing defendants were able to argue that the sentence imposed by the Court would more than adequately address the concerns and that an order was simply not necessary. Unfortunately, the new 'helpful' test has meant that prosecution submissions routinely emphasise that the proposed terms of the CBO will add at least something to the protection otherwise afforded by the sentence imposed on the defendant. This submission frequently finds favour with the Court, resulting in the imposition of a CBO where an application for an ASBO would not have been successful.

There is no burden on the prosecution to demonstrate to any standard that the imposition of the CBO would be helpful under condition two. In DPP *v Bulmer* [2015] EWHC 2323 (Admin), the Administrative

Court confirmed that there was no reference to either a burden or standard of proof in the legislation when addressing the second condition. The Court stated in paragraph 30 of the judgment that "*had Parliament wished the criminal standard to apply, it could have used the appropriate language*" and instead stated that the enquiry under condition two was a matter for the Court's "*judgment and evaluation*".

The second condition represents a significant obstacle for those responding to applications for CBOs. Legal practitioners should focus their submissions on any identifiable limitations within the evidence produced in support of the prosecution application. For example, consider the nature and seriousness of the conduct complained of, any lack of frequency or duration in the behaviour, any suggestion that there has been a limited impact on the community, the unlikelihood of a repetition in the behaviour, an absence / small number of relevant previous convictions / activities and any positive response by the defendant to previous sentences. But the experience of those of us working in this area is that the Court frequently concludes that such orders would be 'helpful'.

Prohibitions and requirements

As previously outlined, the terms of a CBO may impose prohibitions and requirements upon a defendant. The proposed terms must not prohibit conduct which itself constitutes a criminal offence (*Brain* [2020] EWCA Crim 457).

The introduction of positive requirements represented a significant move away from the old ASBO regime where such orders were limited to imposing restrictions and the Court was unable not require the individual to do any positive act. In the context of boys and young men involved in alleged gang activities and the drill music scene, this deliberate widening of the scope of such orders has had a significant impact. Legal practitioners working in this area need to have a comprehensive understanding of the relevant caselaw, particularly the leading authority of *Khan* [2018] EWCA Crim 1472.

In *Khan* the Court of Appeal addressed in detail the approach that ought to be taken by the Court when deciding upon the terms of a CBO. The appellant in *Khan* sought to challenge both the imposition of and the terms set out within the CBO imposed by the Crown Court. The Court of Appeal reviewed the authorities in relation to ASBOs, particularly *Boness* [2005] EWCA Crim 2395, and adopted the same strict approach (paragraph 14):

> *"The terms of the order must be precise and capable of being understood by the offender. The findings of fact giving rise to the making of the order must be recorded. The order must be explained to the offender. The exact terms of the order must be pronounced in open Court and the written order must accurately reflect the order as pronounced"*

The Court of Appeal went further, building on the *Boness* principles, and stated that the judge should consider the following (paragraph 15):

> *"Because an order must be precise and capable of being understood by the offender, a court should ask itself before making an order "Are the terms of this order clear so that the offender will know precisely what it is that he is prohibited from doing?" Prohibitions should be reasonable and proportionate; realistic and practical; and be in terms which make it easy to determine and prosecute a breach. Exclusion zones should be clearly delineated (generally with the use of clearly marked maps, although we do not consider that there is a problem of definition in an order extending to Greater Manchester) and individuals whom the defendant is prohibited from contacting or associating with should be clearly identified. In the case of a foreign national, consideration should be given to the need for the order to be translated."*

It is worth emphasising that the Court of Appeal in *Khan* referred to the wording of the Home Office explanatory note accompanying the legislation introducing CBOs, placing significance upon the description that CBOs were only *"intended for tackling the most serious and persistent offenders where their behaviour has brought them before a criminal court"* (Home Office, *'Anti-Social Behaviour Powers – Statutory Guidance for Frontline Professionals'*, revised March 2023).

It was on that basis that the Court of Appeal in *Khan* adopted, in the context of CBOs, the comments of Lord Justice Beatson in *DPP v Bulmer* [2015] EWHC 2323 (Admin) in relation to ASBOs, specifically stating at paragraph 20 that:

> *"...such orders are not lightly to be imposed; the Court should proceed with a proper degree of caution and circumspection; the order must be tailored to the specific circumstances of the person on whom it is to be imposed and assessments of proportionality are intensely fact-sensitive."*

Legal practitioners working in this area know that success in opposing these applications requires persuasive submissions based on proportionality. Indeed even the Court of Appeal has had cause to quash prohibitions and requirements set out within CBOs that fall foul of the principles set out in *Khan*.

In *Maguire* [2019] EWCA Crim 1193, the Court of Appeal held that a clause in a CBO requiring an individual with a history of domestic violence to 'inform the local police station of the name of any new partner within 14 days of commencing an intimate relationship' was hopelessly vague and not sufficiently clear or capable of being policed. Similarly, in *Brain* [2020] EWCA Crim 457, a blanket ban against the use of any internet based social networking site by an individual was found to inhibit his employment prospects.

When drafting a response legal practitioners ought to have regard to s.331(4) SA 2020, which states that prohibitions and requirements must, *"so far as is practicable"*, avoid:

(a) Any interference with the times, if any, at which the defendant normally works or attends school or any other educational establishment.

(b) Any conflict with the requirements of any other Court order or injunction to which the defendant may be subject.

This particular provision has proven effective on occasion when addressing the Court on behalf of boys and young men engaged in educational and employment schemes. Unfortunately, the provision includes the unhelpful caveat '*so far as is practicable*', which allows the Court a level of discretion even where the terms of an order would interfere with the education and employment of defendants.

This is exemplified by the decision of the Court of Appeal in *Janes* [2016] EWCA Crim 676. The defendant was a self-employed gardener who had committed fraud by overcharging elderly customers. The terms of the CBO included a prohibition preventing him from "*touting*" for business, which he argued interfered with the operation of his business and employment. The Court of Appeal started by helpfully stating that although s.331(4)(a) referred to the "*times*" at which a defendant worked, the wording of the legislation implied that such orders should not prevent an individual from working. For those who represent boys and young men the point would clearly apply equally to school and other educational establishments. However, the Court of Appeal highlighted the inclusion of '*so far as is practicable*' and relied upon that caveat to conclude that there was no reason not to make the CBO given the individual's previous conduct arose out of the performance of his work. The Court of Appeal was of the view that such a term was not capable of engaging article 8 of the ECHR but, even if it were, the term was necessary for the prevention of crime and proportionate in its application (paragraph 18).

In recent years, legal practitioners working in this area will have observed a deliberate movement by first instance judges away from the restrictive, focused approach endorsed in *Khan*. Successfully opposing prosecution applications for CBOs, even when conceding the merits of the order and instead arguing for a more proportionate approach to the terms, has become much harder. This is particularly so when representing boys and young men identified by the police and prosecution as involved in the drill music scene. The terms of the proposed orders can be very restrictive. For example, recent applications for CBOs have included terms prohibiting association with others involved in drill music, prohibiting the material that can be placed on social media, prohibiting reference in drill lyrics and videos to certain names and locations, prohibiting the performance of particular drill songs, prohibiting attendance at music events such as the Notting Hill Carnival and even a requirement that the police are notified in advance of an intention to release any new drill lyrics or videos. Unsurprisingly, legal practitioners frequently oppose the imposition of such terms, arguing that they are not only disproportionate but effectively amount to cultural censorship.

Responding to CBO applications

The Court of Appeal has repeatedly emphasised that "*it was not the intention of Parliament that criminal behaviour orders should become a mere matter of box ticking routine*" (see paragraph 20 of *Khan*). That may well not have been the intention of Parliament when introducing CBOs. However, the provisions have been expansively applied in practice which has, unfortunately, resulted in many cases being rendered box ticking exercises. As previously outlined, this is largely due to the lowering of the legislative thresholds for the steps necessary to make CBOs.

Nevertheless, legal practitioners ought to engage with each aspect of the legislative provisions and mount forceful arguments opposing the imposition of broad, undefined CBOs that have the potential to significantly infringe upon a defendant's human rights. The prosecution and Court ought to be asked whether the CBO is really needed given the cautious approach that should be adopted in accordance with *Khan*. In the context of musical and social media activities, is there sufficient evidence that it is linked to the actual or likely harassment, alarm or distress of others? CBOs should be sparingly made and drafted with careful precision, particularly when the Court is concerned with children and young adults.

PART 4

FUTURE AND REFORM

CHAPTER TWELVE

PROPOSALS FOR FUTURE REFORMS

As outlined in previous chapters, practitioners are increasingly faced with prosecution applications seeking to admit as gang evidence drill lyrics, music videos and other forms of cultural expression as bad character in criminal cases. While the Criminal Justice Act 2003 ('CJA 2003') provides gateways for admitting bad character evidence, the provisions were drafted and passed at a time when social media, digital evidence and musical genres like drill music did not exist in England and Wales. Legal practitioners working in this area will be familiar with the calls for reform, particularly given the perception that the current rules result in unfair prejudice, racial stereotyping and an unjustified restriction on freedom of expression. This chapter seeks to explore the potential areas that may benefit from future reform.

Evidential Thresholds

As outlined in Part 2, the current law in relation to bad character allows for drill lyrics and other forms of expression deemed gang related to be admitted if assessed as relevant e.g. relevant to an important matter in issue under s.101(1)(d) CJA 2003.

Legal practitioners working in this area will be familiar with the criticism that the current relevance test has created too low a starting point for such evidence to be admitted and that frequently the relevant evidence is of minor importance to the overall case. Many argue that this is due to both the prosecution and judiciary failing to handle these points with sufficient knowledge of drill music and other cultural forms of expression. One solution may be to allow them time to catch up, perhaps with the assistance of appropriate training from the Crown Prosecution Service and Judicial College. However, despite this issue having been a live one for many years and considered in a significant number of Court of Appeal cases, there has been little judicial movement towards a greater appreciation for the nuance of drill music. Therefore, the time might have come for reform by way of exclusion of such evidence.

The starting point for any new legislation or legal principle may be to introduce a presumption against the admission of any evidence that amounts to creative expression. This may include, but should not be limited to, drill lyrics, music videos, films and other forms of cultural expression e.g. poetry. The presumption, like many within the criminal justice system, could be rebuttable where the prosecution is able to demonstrate there is a direct nexus between the material and the alleged offending in the criminal case.

Such an approach to controversial areas of evidence, where there is a risk of jurors being influenced by harmful stereotypes, is not without precedent in our criminal justice system. For example, s.41 of the Youth Justice and Criminal Evidence Act 1999, affords protection to complainants by restricting evidence or questions from the defence about their previous sexual history unless one of a series of specific exceptions is satisfied and the Court grants leave. The purpose of that legislation was to deal with the myth that because a woman has had sexual intercourse on occasions other than those covered by the criminal case this increases the probability that she consented to intercourse with the accused; a harmful myth that relied upon unfounded stereotypes and prejudices. The presumption against the admission of any evidence of creative expression, such material having been shown to result in inappropriate racial stereotyping, would work in a similar way.

Any legislation introduced in this area ought to address the specific position in relation to those aged under 18. Legal practitioners working in this area know that the danger associated with relying on the content of drill lyrics is particularly high when dealing with child defendants. The content of the material tends to include more instances of bravado and exaggeration, typically because these young individuals have little experience of either the real world or gang activities and seek to inflate their own standing within the community. Therefore, it may be appropriate to legislate that any evidence of creative expression by those under 18 should be excluded unless there are exceptional circumstances e.g. material amounts to a clear confession of the offence. It would also assist if the Crown Prosecution Service were to review and amend their guidance in relation to such applications, perhaps to limit the frequency with which such applications are made in relation to those under 18 e.g. applications should only be made where the child is accused of the most serious offences such as murder. Such an approach by both the judiciary and the prosecution would likely go some way to showing those typically targeted by applications to adduce gang evidence, namely black boys and young men, that the criminal justice system is not set up to work against them and instead adopts a scrupulously fair and proportionate approach in each individual case.

Finally in relation to the evidential threshold, consideration ought to be given to a statutory amendment to the bad character provisions requiring the Court to specifically consider the human rights implications of criminalising creative expression in the form of material such as drill lyrics. Legal practitioners know that the potential interference with the freedom of expression (Article 10) is not widely considered when dealing with applications to adduce gang evidence. The Court tends to focus rather narrowly on the balance between the probative value of the material and the prejudicial effect of allowing it to go before the jury. The potential impact of using such material to support a criminal prosecution, in particular whether it amounts to a proportionate interference with the freedom of expression by those in the relevant community, is not frequently raised or considered by the Court. For example, is it proportionate to use such material to prosecute individuals given the inevitable consequence that it will discourage cultural expression within an already disenfranchised community? Many argue that there should be a place for consideration of these human rights issues, and that it should be reflected in the legislation, when deciding upon the admissibility of gang evidence and drill lyrics.

Standards for Experts

As outlined in Chapter 6, prosecution applications frequently rely upon police officers as so called 'gang experts'. The source of this expertise is often limited in its detail and unquantifiable for the defence. The criticism is often made by defence teams that police officers, with their expertise based entirely on law enforcement, are not best placed to provide expertise on what is essentially highly specific cultural material. Frequently, police officers called as experts tasked with the interpretation of alleged gang evidence, such as the content of drill lyrics, make mistakes, misread slang or undertake a selective interpretation of the text resulting in the presentation of an entirely false narrative.

To address these concerns, one solution would be to establish an official accreditation scheme for individuals who seek to promote themselves as gang experts able to interpret drill lyrics and music. To ensure that high standards are achieved and maintained, the accreditation body ought to be independent of both prosecution and defence organisations. The accreditation body's primary task would be to ensure that all experts are independent and transparent in their methodology.

Building on the creation of an accreditation body, the Court process could be adapted to ensure that any prosecution expert evidence is not only considered at an early stage in proceedings but is automatically subjected to consideration by either a defence expert or Court appointed expert. This could be built into the current stage date process adopted in the Crown Court and would adopt an approach like that taken when addressing expert evidence on the issue of a defendant's fitness to plead and stand trial. Such a process would have the benefit of not only neutralising the often adversarial approach taken by parties but would also ensure that proper expertise is relied upon and is open to challenge in pre-trial hearings designed to focus on the admissibility of such evidence.

Finally, and most importantly, the Court could supplement the current 'relevance' test with a new standard of 'reliability' when deciding whether to admit expert evidence on gangs and drill lyrics. This would require any expert relied upon by either the prosecution or defence to establish that their evidence is reliable by reference to verifiable methodology. This is not without precedent and the Court would be invited to adopt an approach like that established in the United States of America in *Daubert* (1993) 509 U.S. 579. In that case the United States Supreme Court stated that the conclusion of a witness would only qualify as scientific knowledge (or expert evidence) if that witness could demonstrate that it was the product of sound 'scientific methodology', which was defined as the process of formulating hypotheses and then conducting experiments to prove of falsify the hypothesis. Adopting a similar approach with gang evidence and drill lyrics in England and Wales, the Court may seek to ask the following questions:

- Is the theory or technique employed by the expert generally accepted in the wider expert community?

- Has the theory or technique been subjected to peer review and publication?

- Can the theory or technique be tested? If so, has it been tested?

- Does the theory or technique have a known error rate?

- Was the research conducted independent of the criminal case or dependent on an intention to provide evidence in the criminal case?

The adoption of a reliability test would ensure that the expertise of the individual, whether a police officer, musician, industry insider or academic specialising in drill music and culture, would be beyond question. It would build on the frequently ignored Criminal Procedure Rules and Criminal Practice Direction dealing with expert evidence. Such an approach would also ensure a more transparent process allowing all parties to more effectively assess and challenge the evidence before the Court is invited to make a final decision on admissibility.

Jury Directions

As discussed in earlier chapters of this book, there is an obvious risk that jurors may unconsciously equate evidence of cultural expression in the form of drill lyrics with criminality. That is likely a consequence of the approach taken by both politicians and the national media when discussing this type of material. Therefore, judicial directions to the jury about gang evidence and drill lyrics need to address the risk.

Unfortunately, legal practitioners instructed in these cases know that such judicial directions are frequently minimal at best and often do not specifically address the issue of cultural expression or advise caution when considering evidence such as drill lyrics. For example, the legal direction will often state something generic about gang evidence, warn that the word 'gang' has negative connotations but that the jury must avoid relying on false assumptions, stereotypes and prejudices.

The issue could be addressed by the Judicial College putting together a draft model direction to be included in the Crown Court Compendium that specifically warns jurors about the risks associated with conflating artistic expression in the form of drill lyrics / music with an autobiographical confession. The jury could be explicitly reminded that many art forms, not just rap and drill music, rely upon exaggeration, metaphors and provocative language.

The proposed direction might be drafted in the following terms:

> *"You have heard drill lyrics / music during this trial. All parties agree that these are forms of artistic expression and must be approached with caution. Such lyrics / music often relies upon exaggeration, metaphors and provocative language. The performers routinely engage in role-play and adopt stage personas that may be untrue. You must not assume that performing or writing those words means that the defendant lived them out or that they represent their personal experiences or intentions. You may only use those words as evidence against the defendant if you are sure that they are directly relevant to the facts of this case. Even if you are so sure it does not necessarily follow that they are guilty of the offence."*

The adoption of this type of standard direction in cases where drill lyrics / music has gone before the jury may be thought to be a good starting point.

Conclusion

The future trajectory of gang evidence and drill lyrics in criminal proceedings raises important discussions about culture, freedom and fairness. If there is to be a review of the relevant law in this area, future reform should not be simply limited to technical evidential tweaks. The widespread criticism justifies a careful consideration of the potential systemic bias built into the process and ought to seek to recalibrate the balance that has thus far been struck between probative value on one hand and prejudice to the individual on the other.

Any future attempts to reform this area of law ought to be based on proper research and analysis. This would ideally be undertaken by either the Law Commission or by a suitably qualified Parliamentary group such as the Justice Committee with significant input from practitioners, artists and NGOs. The research ought to specifically consider jury comprehension and bias in cases where they are tasked with considering gang evidence and drill lyrics. The research would then guide those tasked with legislating any future reforms in this area.

MORE BOOKS BY LAW BRIEF PUBLISHING

A selection of our other titles available now:-

'A Practical Guide to Probation Breaches and Other Applications' by Mark Thomas
'A Practical Guide to Remarriage and Divorce' by Cordelia Williams & Claire Howard
'A Practical Guide to Privacy, Transparency, Reporting Restrictions and Closed Proceedings in the Court of Protection' by Laura Mannering
'Beaumont on Barristers – A Guide to Defending Disciplinary Proceedings (Second Edition)' by Marc Beaumont
'A Practical Guide to Payments for Environmental Services' by Ben Sharples
'A Practical Guide to the Law of Pregnancy and Maternity at Work' by Rebecca Thomas
'A Practical Guide to Redundancy – Second Edition' by Philip Hyland & Collette Moore
'A Practical Guide to International Issues for Scottish Family Lawyers' by Susie Mountain, Donna McKay, Ken MacDonald
'A Practical Guide to the Law on Deprivation of Liberty' by Ben Troke
'A Practical Guide to Rights over Airspace and Subsoil – Second Edition' by Daniel Gatty
'A Practical Guide to the Law in Relation to Inquests' by Ramya Nagesh
'A Practical Guide to the Construction and Rectification of Wills and Trust Instruments (Second Edition)' by Edward Hewitt
'A Practical Guide to Data Protection in Social Housing' by Clare Paterson
'A Practical Guide to Spousal Maintenance – Second Edition' by Liz Cowell
'A Practical Guide to International Parental Child Abduction Law (England and Wales)' by Dr Onyója Momoh
'A Practical Guide to Deprivation of British Citizenship' by Sean Ell
'A Practical Guide to Commercial Property Service Charges' by Rachel Garton
'A Practical Guide to Clinical Negligence – Third Edition' by Geoffrey Simpson-Scott (Geoff)
'A Practical Guide to the Rights of Grandparents in Children Proceedings – Second Edition' by Stuart Barlow

'The Electronic Communications Code: A Practical Guide – Second Edition' by Kerry Bretherton KC, James Castle, Mark Loveday
'A Practical Guide to the Independent School Standards – September 2023 Edition' by Sarah McKimm
'A Practical Guide to Estate Administration and Crypto Assets' by Richard Marshall
'A Practical Guide to Parental Alienation in Private and Public Law Children Cases' by Sam King QC & Frankie Shama
'Contested Heritage – Removing Art from Land and Historic Buildings' by Richard Harwood QC, Catherine Dobson, David Sawtell
'The Limits of Separate Legal Personality: When Those Running a Company Can Be Held Personally Liable for Losses Caused to Third Parties Outside of the Company' by Dr Mike Wilkinson
'A Practical Guide to Transgender Law' by Robin Moira White & Nicola Newbegin
'A Practical Guide to 'Stranded Spouses' in Family Law' by Mani Singh Basi
'A Practical Guide to Residential Freehold Conveyancing' by Lorraine Richardson
'A Practical Guide to Pensions on Divorce for Lawyers' by Bryan Scant
'A Practical Guide to Challenging Sham Marriage Allegations in Immigration Law' by Priya Solanki
'A Practical Guide to Digital Communications Evidence in Criminal Law' by Sam Willis
'A Practical Guide to Legal Rights in Scotland' by Sarah-Jane Macdonald
'A Practical Guide to New Build Conveyancing' by Paul Sams & Rebecca East
'A Practical Guide to Inherited Wealth on Divorce' by Hayley Trim
'A Practical Guide to Practice Direction 12J and Domestic Abuse in Private Law Children Proceedings' by Rebecca Cross & Malvika Jaganmohan
'A Practical Guide to Confiscation and Restraint' by Narita Bahra QC, John Carl Townsend, David Winch
'A Practical Guide to the Law of Forests in Scotland' by Philip Buchan
'A Practical Guide to Health and Medical Cases in Immigration Law' by Rebecca Chapman & Miranda Butler
'A Practical Guide to Bad Character Evidence for Criminal Practitioners by Aparna Rao
'A Practical Guide to Extradition Law post-Brexit' by Myles Grandison et al
'A Practical Guide to Hoarding and Mental Health for Housing Lawyers' by Rachel Coyle

'Stephens on Contractual Indemnities' by Richard Stephens
'A Practical Guide to the EU Succession Regulation' by Richard Frimston
'A Practical Guide to Solicitor and Client Costs – Second Edition' by Robin Dunne
'Constructive Dismissal – Practice Pointers and Principles' by Benjimin Burgher
'A Practical Guide to Religion and Belief Discrimination Claims in the Workplace' by Kashif Ali
'A Practical Guide to the Law of Medical Treatment Decisions' by Ben Troke
'Fundamental Dishonesty and QOCS in Personal Injury Proceedings: Law and Practice' by Jake Rowley
'A Practical Guide to the Law in Relation to School Exclusions' by Charlotte Hadfield & Alice de Coverley
'A Practical Guide to Divorce for the Silver Separators' by Karin Walker
'The Right to be Forgotten – The Law and Practical Issues' by Melissa Stock
'A Practical Guide to Planning Law and Rights of Way in National Parks, the Broads and AONBs' by James Maurici QC, James Neill et al
'A Practical Guide to Election Law' by Tom Tabori
'A Practical Guide to the Law in Relation to Surrogacy' by Andrew Powell
'A Practical Guide to Claims Arising from Fatal Accidents – Second Edition' by James Patience
'A Practical Guide to Asbestos Claims' by Jonathan Owen & Gareth McAloon
'A Practical Guide to Stamp Duty Land Tax in England and Northern Ireland' by Suzanne O'Hara
'A Practical Guide to the Law of Farming Partnerships' by Philip Whitcomb
'A Practical Guide to the Law of Unlawful Eviction and Harassment – Second Edition' by Stephanie Lovegrove
'A Practical Guide to Costs in Personal Injury Claims – Second Edition' by Matthew Hoe
'A Practical Guide to the General Data Protection Regulation (GDPR) – Second Edition' by Keith Markham
'A Practical Guide to Working with Litigants in Person and McKenzie Friends in Family Cases' by Stuart Barlow
'Protecting Unregistered Brands: A Practical Guide to the Law of Passing Off' by Lorna Brazell
'A Practical Guide to Secondary Liability and Joint Enterprise Post-Jogee' by Joanne Cecil & James Mehigan

'A Practical Guide to the Pre-Action RTA Claims Protocol for Personal Injury Lawyers' by Antonia Ford
'A Practical Guide to Neighbour Disputes and the Law' by Alexander Walsh
'A Practical Guide to Coercive Control for Legal Practitioners and Victims' by Rachel Horman
'A Practical Guide to the Law of Driverless Cars – Second Edition'
by Alex Glassbrook, Emma Northey & Scarlett Milligan
'A Practical Guide to TOLATA Claims' by Greg Williams
'A Practical Guide to Elderly Law – Second Edition' by Justin Patten
'A Practical Guide to Responding to Housing Disrepair and Unfitness Claims' by Iain Wightwick
'A Practical Guide to the Law of Bullying and Harassment in the Workplace' by Philip Hyland
'How to Be a Freelance Solicitor: A Practical Guide to the SRA-Regulated Freelance Solicitor Model' by Paul Bennett
'A Practical Guide to Prison Injury Claims' by Malcolm Johnson
'A Practical Guide to Advising Clients at the Police Station' by Colin Stephen McKeown-Beaumont
'A Practical Guide to Antisocial Behaviour Injunctions – Second Edition' by Iain Wightwick
'Practical Mediation: A Guide for Mediators, Advocates, Advisers, Lawyers, and Students in Civil, Commercial, Business, Property, Workplace, and Employment Cases' by Jonathan Dingle with John Sephton
'The Mini-Pupillage Workbook' by David Boyle
'A Practical Guide to Crofting Law' by Brian Inkster
'A Practical Guide to the Law of Domain Names and Cybersquatting' by Andrew Clemson
'A Practical Guide to the Law of Gender Pay Gap Reporting' by Harini Iyengar
'NHS Whistleblowing and the Law' by Joseph England
'Employment Law and the Gig Economy' by Nigel Mackay & Annie Powell
'A Practical Guide to Noise Induced Hearing Loss (NIHL) Claims' by Andrew Mckie, Ian Skeate, Gareth McAloon
'An Introduction to Beauty Negligence Claims – A Practical Guide for the Personal Injury Practitioner' by Greg Almond
'Intercompany Agreements for Transfer Pricing Compliance' by Paul Sutton
'Zen and the Art of Mediation' by Martin Plowman
'A Practical Guide to Adoption for Family Lawyers' by Graham Pegg

'A Practical Guide to Industrial Disease Claims' by Andrew Mckie & Ian Skeate
'A Practical Guide to Conducting a Sheriff Court Proof' by Andrew Stevenson
'A Practical Guide to Vicarious Liability' by Mariel Irvine
'A Practical Guide to Applications for Landlord's Consent and Variation of Leases' by Mark Shelton
'A Practical Guide to Relief from Sanctions Post-Mitchell and Denton' by Peter Causton
'A Practical Guide to Equity Release for Advisors' by Paul Sams
'A Practical Guide to Financial Services Claims' by Chris Hegarty
'A Practical Guide to Financial Ombudsman Service Claims' by Adam Temple & Robert Scrivenor
'A Practical Guide to Running Housing Disrepair and Cavity Wall Claims – Second Edition' by Andrew Mckie & Ian Skeate
'A Practical Guide to Holiday Sickness Claims – Second Edition' by Andrew Mckie & Ian Skeate
'Arguments and Tactics for Personal Injury and Clinical Negligence Claims' by Dorian Williams
'A Practical Guide to Drone Law' by Rufus Ballaster, Andrew Firman, Eleanor Clot
'On Experts: CPR35 for Lawyers and Experts' by David Boyle
'An Introduction to Personal Injury Law' by David Boyle

www.ingramcontent.com/pod-product-compliance
Lightning Source LLC
LaVergne TN
LVHW022107200926
848481LV00003B/1085

9781918241075